SPRINTS
AND REL

by Frank W. Dick, O.B.E.

(B.A.A.B. Director of Coaching)

Sprinting and Relay Racing
First published 1959 (J.W.Ll. Alford and A.R. Malcolm)
Second Edition 1966 (W. Marlow)
Third Edition 1972 (W. Marlow)
Fourth Edition 1977 (W. Marlow)
Fifth Edition under present title 1987 (F. Dick)
This Edition 1991 (F. Dick)

Dear Coach,

This book is dedicated to, and written for, you — the sprints coach or coach to athletes in speed dependent events and sports. I hope there's something here for each one of you, because not only did you inspire me to write it — you helped produce its content by letting me be a beneficiary of your experience.

Achievement for the athlete is total personal expression in the arena in reaching for his or her competition goal. Achievement for the coach is also total personal expression in directing the athlete's talents and motivations towards that goal. The coach requires, then, a very special blend of personal skills and values born of a creative passion. The good coach is, moreover, just as achievement orientated as the athlete. It has been my good fortune to have been helped by many other coaches to achieve my coaching goals. This booket will, I hope, help you.

I wish you well in pursuit of all the achievement you deserve, through your study, hard work, dedication, and creative passion.

Dear Athlete,

Your talent, hard work, patience and commitment to success are sound foundations for the success you deserve. It's up to you to ensure that the success you deserve is the success you want.

Although yours is the excitement of competition, the fulfilment of winning and the lessons of losing, yours also is the role of ambassador for British Athletics, whether you are club athlete or Olympian. This is both privilege and responsibility. Your approach to life on and off the track will be viewed as a reflection of this.

Respect your opponent at all times. His endeavours push you to greater things; and when the contest is over, acknowledge your appreciation of those qualities he brings to the arena.

Each competition requires the expert service of officials who organise, arbitrate and record the event. It is they who provide occasion for competition and ensure the fairness of the contest you require. You should make a point of thanking them for that service when opportunity occurs to do so.

Believe in your coach; in your programme; in the values of your sport; and in the way you interpret those values in your lifestyle. But more important still, believe in you.

I hope this booklet will help you in pursuit of your athletic ambitions; that the sport will afford you unique opportunity to express your abilities; and that athletics will be the richer for your contribution.

ABOUT THE AUTHOR

Frank Dick is the B.A.A.B. Director of Coaching, President of the European Athletics Coaches' Association and Chairman of the British Olympic Association's Coaching Advisory Group. He studied at Edinburgh University, Loughborough and the University of Oregon, and is a former Fulbright Scholar. His detailed study of training principles and practice has established him as a leading international authority in Training Theory and in the synthesis of sports science for coaches.

An international athlete himself, he has coached athletes to Olympic, World and European honours in several events. His specialist area is, however, the sprints, and since he took charge of the International Relay teams in 1978, Britain has enjoyed an unprecedented period of international success.

Acknowledgements

I acknowledge with gratitude and respect the contribution of athletes and coaching colleagues to the content of this booklet.

In particular, I would like to thank

Bill Marlow;	Mike Smith;	Iain Robertson;
Jim Bradley;	John Isaacs;	John Anderson;
Wilson Young;	Carlo Vittori;	Horst-Dieter Hille.

I wish to thank David Cocksedge, Helmar Hommel, Howard Payne and Mark Shearman for their help in kindly supplying photographs.

I would also like to record my appreciation to my former secretary, Diana Bates and present secretary, Melanie James, for translating my handwriting into type; Barry Willis for his counsel and editing; and the B.A.A.B. for making this publication possible.

Finally, I am most grateful to Stan Greenberg and Peter Matthews for access to their expertise in checking statistics.

Contents

TABLES

1.00 INTRODUCTION

The sprinter's objective has been very simply stated — "I want to get from here to there.... first!". The events are the shortest track races and embrace both relays. The distances are 100m, 200m, 400m, 4 × 100m and 4 × 400m. Indoors, 100m is replaced by 50m or 60m; and when a relay is part of the programme, it is normally 4 × 400m — with 4 × 200m occasionally included.

For age group athletes, it is unreasonable to expect any but the exceptional to view 400m as a sprint event! For them the concept of sprinting is lost when the event appears more endurance than speed, and for this reason the favoured competition distances for the majority of age group athletes are 60m-100m, and 150m-200m. For them, the longer events — 300-400m will normally tend to be more relevant to athletes whose future rests in middle to long distance.

Although the sprints are events in themselves, the ability to sprint is critical to successful performance in the majority of athletics events — and it is clearly a determining factor in many sports. No athlete involved in such events or sports can omit specific sprint work from his training programme.

2.00 OVERVIEW OF EVENTS AND STANDARDS

2.10 100m

The winner of the 100m at major international meetings is accorded the accolade "The fastest athlete". The title suggests that the event is considered as the Blue Riband speed event. A sprinter, whether 100m, 200m or 400m, aims to "be first" and/or to reduce his personal best "legal" time. This assault on time is first by seconds, then by tenths, then by hundredths. This athlete appreciates a following wind of up to 2.00m/sec.

Whilst a stronger following wind will certainly blow him or her to faster "illegal" times, the athlete in "windy" conditions tends to consider the result more than the time. The things he loves most are warm temperatures, legal tail winds, dry conditions and prompt "clean" starts. He or she hates multiple starts due to athletes "breaking", guns jamming etc, suspect blocks, electrical timing equipment that breaks down, and the absence of — or a faulty — wind gauge.

If the zenith of achievement in terms of result is an Olympic, World, European or Commonwealth Gold — the zenith of achievement in terms of performance must be "evens". "Evens" for men is running 100m in 10 sec; the equivalent for women is running 100m in 11 secs. (Table 1)

Such athletes are, of course, all time "super-class" — especially when you consider that less than 30 female athletes have run inside 11.10; and less than 30 male athletes have run inside 10.10. To date, for U.K., only Kathy Cook has produced this level of performance — 11.10 when running second to Evelyn Ashford, ahead of Marlies Gohr, in the 1981 World Cup. Linford Christie is the only U.K. male athlete to run inside 10.10 when winning the 1988 Olympic Silver Medal. Allan Wells came very close at 10.11 when winning his semi-final in Moscow — before going on to take the 1980 Gold Medal. Only one other Briton has won an Olympic 100m Gold — Harold Abrahams in 1924. U.K. sprinters can consider themselves in an élite "club" when running inside 10.30 (men) or inside 11.30 (women). Athletes of this class have made serious and often successful challenge for medals at Olympic, World, European, World Student and Commonwealth levels. This select "club" is currently as table 2.

TABLE 1
"EVENS ATHLETES" 100m

As of 31st December 1990
MALE 10.00 or better

9.92	Carl Lewis	USA	1988
9.93A (9.97)	Calvin Smith	USA	1983
9.94	Leroy Burrell	USA	1989
9.95	Ben Johnson	CAN	1986
9.95A (10.03)	Jim Hines	USA	1968
9.96	Mel Lattany	USA	1984
9.97	Linford Christie	GBR	1988
9.97	Ray Stewart	JAM	1989
9.98A (10.03)	Silvio Leonard	CUB	1977
10.00	Marian Woronin	POL	1984
10.00	Chidi Imoh	NGR	1986
10.00	Robson da Silva	BRA	1988

FEMALE 11.00 or better

10.49	Florence Griffith-Joyner	USA	1988
10.76	Evelyn Ashford	USA	1984
10.78A (10.91)	Dawn Sowell	USA	1989
10.78	Merlene Ottey	JAM	1990
10.81	Marlies Gohr	GDR	1983
10.83	Marita Koch	GDR	1983
10.83	Sheila Echols	USA	1988
10.85	Anelia Nuneva	BUL	1988
10.86	Silke Moller	GDR	1987
10.89	Katrin Krabbe	GDR	1990
10.91	Heike Drechsler	GDR	1986
10.91	Gwen Torrence	USA	1988
10.92	Alice Brown	USA	1988
10.93	Eva Kasprzyk	POL	1986
10.94A (11.00)	Diane Williams	USA	1983
10.95	Barbel Wockel	GDR	1982
10.97	Angella Issajenko	CAN	1987
10.97	Gail Devers	USA	1988
10.98	Marina Zhirova	URS	1985
10.98	Angela Bailey	CAN	1988
10.98	Natalya Pomoshnikova	URS	1988
10.99	Valerie Brisco-Hooks	USA	1986

A = Altitude performance

TABLE 2

U.K. MEN 100m			U.K. WOMEN 100m		
Linford Christie	9.97	1988	Kathy Cook	11.10	1981
Allan Wells	10.11	1980	Andrea Lynch	11.16	1975
Cameron Sharp	10.20	1983	Sonia Lannaman	11.20	1980
Elliot Bunney	10.20	1986	Heather Oakes	11.20	1980
John Regis	10.20	1990	Bev Callender	11.22A	1979
Ainsley Bennett	10.21A	1979	Paula Dunn	11.25	1986
Jamie Henderson	10.21	1987	Bev Kinch	11.29	1990
Mike McFarlane	10.22	1986			
Daley Thompson	10.26	1986			
Ernest Obeng	10.26	1987			
Marcus Adam	10.28	1989			
Darren Braithwaite	10.28	1990			
Peter Radford	10.29	1958			
Colin Jackson	10.29	1990			

Table 3 represents the U.K. 1st, 3rd, 6th and 10th performance each year since 1980. It gives some indication not only of the relative improvement of performance in the U.K., but also of the standards required of athletes to move into the U.K. National "Pool".

TABLE 3
U.K. PERFORMANCE 100m

MEN

U.K.

Ranking	1980	1981	1982	1983	1984	1985	1986	1987	1988	1989	1990
1	10.11	10.17	10.20	10.15	10.18	10.31	10.04	10.03	9.97	10.10	10.02
3	10.40	10.47	10.37	10.32	10.32	10.38	10.22	10.25	10.34	10.39	10.25
6	10.51	10.50	10.48	10.42	10.40	10.46	10.32	10.34	10.38	10.44	10.29
10	10.61	10.55	10.54	10.56	10.49	10.61	10.46	10.37	10.45	10.48	10.44

WOMEN

U.K.

Ranking	1980	1981	1982	1983	1984	1985	1986	1987	1988	1989	1990
1	11.20	11.10	11.31	11.13	11.24	11.33	11.22	11.27	11.26	11.24	11.29
3	11.24	11.47	11.36	11.31	11.39	11.42	11.50	11.39	11.50	11.49	11.46
6	11.57	11.69	11.46	11.41	11.50	11.57	11.59	11.52	11.59	11.64	11.54
10	11.85	11.78	11.52	11.59	11.59	11.67	11.74	11.63	11.72	11.76	11.70

A performance of 10.70 (men) and 11.80 (Women) will normally afford a U.K. athlete top 20 status; whilst a performance of 11.10 (junior men) and 12.20 (intermediate women) is a reasonable indication that an athlete is moving in the right direction for serious sprint ambitions as a senior; or again, 11.40 (youths) and 12.50 (junior girls) are useful marks for athletes at beginner/developing level. When boys are ducking under 12.00 secs. and girls under 13.00 secs. they can think of themselves as sprinters. It should be said, however, that for athletes to be outside such times as they progress through their teens does not mean that they should take up dominoes! They can and will run faster given good coaching, a sound training programme, and an appropriate level of competition.

The event is started from a crouch start — using blocks. The first 20m to 30m is the start of the race. These are *driving* strides as the athlete feels his foot push the track behind him. The next 40m is the main body of the run — the *pick-up* phase as the athlete continues accelerating to full speed, with a full *striding* or *striking* sprint action. The remainder of the race is the finish with the athlete in full flight *holding* form, striding without straining — or building into a *lifting* action of the knees as he aims to surge *beyond* the line. The idea of three variations of sprint technique — DRIVING — STRIDING — LIFTING will be examined in more detail in the technique section. In a very close finish, an athlete might "dip" (or lean further forward) in his last stride to and over the line.

2.20 200m

In age group athletics, at 90% of meetings, the athlete who wins the 100m completes a "double" with the 200m. At the top level, however, although some athletes can still achieve this (e.g. at Olympic Games, Borzov 1972; Lewis 1984; Rudolph 1960; Stecher 1972) it is clear that the trend is for specialists in the 100m or 200m. 100m specialists would include Mel Lattany, Jim Hines, Haseley Crawford and Marlies Gohr. 200m specialists would include Pietro Mennea, Don Quarrie, Tommy Smith and Barbel Wockel. This said, a specialist in one event will normally approach similar "status" in the other.

The idea of "evens" is carried into 200m as 20 secs for men; 22 secs for women.

TABLE 4
"EVENS ATHLETES" 200m

As of 31st December 1990

MALE 20.00 or better

19.72A (19.96)	Pietro Mennea	ITA	1979
19.75	Carl Lewis	USA	1983
19.75	Joe DeLoach	USA	1988
19.83A	Tommie Smith	USA	1968
19.85	Michael Johnson	USA	1990
19.86A	Don Quarrie	JAM	1971
19.87	Lorenzo Daniel	USA	1988
19.92A	John Carlos	USA	1968
19.95	Floyd Heard	USA	1987
19.96	Kirk Baptiste	USA	1984
19.96	Robson da Silva	BRA	1989
19.99	Calvin Smith	USA	1983
20.00	Valeriy Borzov	URS	1972

FEMALE 22.00 or better

21.34	Florence Griffith-Joyner	USA	1988
21.66	Merlene Ottey	JAM	1990
21.71	Marita Koch	GDR	1979
21.71	Heike Drechsler	GDR	1986
21.72	Grace Jackson	JAM.	1988
21.74	Marlies Gohr	GDR	1984
21.74	Silke Moller	GDR	1987
21.81	Valerie Brisco-Hooks	USA	1984
21.83	Evelyn Ashford	USA	1984
21.85	Barbel Wockel	GDR	1984
21.93	Pam Marshall	USA	1988
21.95	Katrin Krabbe	GDR	1990
21.97	Jarmila Kratochvilova	TCH	1981
21.99	Chandra Cheeseborough	USA	1983

A = Altitude performance

Again, these athletes represent all time "super-class" — when considered in the light of less than 30 male athletes running inside 20.20 and less than 30 female athletes running inside 22.40. Kathy Cook's 22.10 in the Los Angeles Olympic Final puts her as the only U.K. athlete in this class. Linford Christie (20.09) and John Regis (20.11) are the only Britons to run inside 20.20. Allan Wells is only just outside with his 20.21 run for second place in Moscow 1980. Only Walter Rangeley — in 1928 — had previously achieved a British Olympic Silver in this event. No other Briton, however, has matched Wells' feat in winning a Gold and Silver in the two sprints.

U.K. sprinters can consider themselves in an élite "club" when running inside 20.60 (men) and 22.80 (women). Athletes of this class have enjoyed considerable success at Olympic, World, European, World Student and Commonwealth levels. This select "club" as of 31/12/90 is as in Table 5.

TABLE 5

U.K. MEN 200m			**U.K. WOMEN 200m**		
Linford Christie	20.09	1988	Kathy Cook	22.10	1984
John Regis	20.11	1990	Sonia Lannaman	22.58	1980
Allan Wells	20.21	1980	Bev Callender	22.72	1980
Todd Bennett	20.36*	1984	Donna Hartley	22.75*	1978
Ainsley Bennett	20.42A	1979	Paula Dunn	22.79	1988
Mike McFarlane	20.43	1982	Michelle Scutt	22.80*	1982
Cameron Sharp	20.47	1982			
Michael Rosswess	20.51	1988			
Ade Mafe	20.54	1985			
Roger Black	20.60*	1990			

* main event at Major Competitions — 400m

Table 6 represents U.K. 1st, 3rd, 6th and 10th performances each year since 1980. It gives some indication of relative improvement of performance in the U.K. — and serves as a guide to the standard required to move into the U.K. National "Pool".

A performance of 21.50 (men) and 24.20 (women) is normally sufficient for an athlete's inclusion in the U.K. top 20; whilst a performance of 22.20 (junior men) and 25.20 (intermediate women) is a reasonable indication that an athlete is moving in the right direction for a promising future in 200m — and/or 400m; or again 22.80 (youths) and 25.80 (junior girls) are useful indices. As a starting point for athletes at beginner/developing level, when boys are running under 25.00 and girls under 28.00 they can begin to think of concentrating attention on the half lap and lap races. Improvement will come as for 100m — with good coaching, a sound training programme, and an appropriate level of competition. What must be said, however, is that the young sprinter should not run 200's if he sees the event as a short endurance race as opposed to a long sprint! As a rule of thumb, athletes should be running around 12 secs (male) and 13 secs (female) for 100m before 200m is given any serious consideration for specialist development.

The event is started from a crouch start using blocks. The first 40m is the *start* of the race with the athlete using a *driving* stride as in 100m. For the next 40m the athlete holds or gently builds on the speed acquired in the first 40m by using the *striding* technique as described for the middle portion of the 100m. The next 30m-40m brings he athlete through the 3rd relay change markings on the track using a *lifting* action to produce the momentum he or she requires for the home straight — where the "long finish" features the striding technique again.

This event must not be viewed by athlete or coach as a flat out 100m followed by 100m "hanging on"! Maximum effort cannot be sustained throughout the distance. There has to be a very carefully thought out distribution of effort. Like the 100m sprinter, this athlete needs conditions where there is a following wind in the home straight up to, but not over, the legal limit of 2.00m/sec. Ideally, any wind should blow diagonally across the stadium from 200m start towards the common finish!

The things he or she hates are as for the 100m athlete — but in addition, Lane 1 is not the most popular — fast followed by Lane 8! The worst possible wind blows diagonally from the common finish towards the 200m start. Races run in such conditions favour the 400m athletes rather than the short sprinter.

TABLE 6
U.K. PERFORMANCE 200m

MEN

U.K.

Ranking	1980	1981	1982	1983	1984	1985	1986	1987	1988	1989	1990
1	20.21	20.26	20.43	20.52	20.36	20.54	20.41	20.18	20.09	20.35	20.11
3	20.81	20.84	20.47	20.77	20.62	20.85	20.51	20.80	20.51	20.62	20.60
6	20.92	21.10	20.88	20.92	20.86	20.97	20.81	20.92	20.90	20.91	20.67
10	21.30	21.24	21.18	21.00	20.93	21.10	21.12	21.08	21.17	21.18	20.89

WOMEN

U.K.

Ranking	*1980*	*1981*	*1982*	*1983*	*1984*	*1985*	*1986*	*1987*	*1988*	*1989*	*1990*
1	22.31	22.58	22.13	22.26	22.10	22.87	22.92	23.17	22.79	23.27	23.07
3	22.72	23.14	22.91	23.07	22.98	23.60	23.35	23.57	23.47	23.43	23.33
6	23.43	23.46	23.19	23.26	23.33	23.65	23.39	23.68	23.69	23.64	23.45
10	23.71	23.94	23.46	23.35	23.50	23.89	23.82	23.79	23.91	23.78	23.59

2.30   400m

The 400m and 400m hurdles athletes must come close to the title "the hardest track athletes". These athletes require to express their running ability with very high levels of strength, of speed and of endurance. Such an athlete prefers warm, dry, windless conditions; but if there is a wind, he likes it behind him for the first part of the race. Lane preference is as for 200m athletes. In addition, likes and dislikes are very much as per the 100m athletes.

The idea of "evens" in 400m would suggest targets of 44 secs — male and 48 secs — female. The only sub 44.00 sec. performances presently recorded have been achieved by Butch Reynolds (USA) 43.29, Lee Evans (USA) 43.86, Steve Lewis (USA) 43.87, Larry James (USA) 43.97 and Danny Everett (USA) 43.98. The only female athletes to go below 48.00 secs to date are Marita Koch (GDR) — 47.60, and Jarmila Kratochvilova (CZECH) — 47.99. Doubtless more athletes will join them but it is clear that at present these targets represent a greater order of difficulty than the 100m and 200m equivalents. A more reasonable "super class" standard would be 44.40 (male) and 49.50 (female). (Table 7).

TABLE 7
ALL TIME TOP PERFORMANCES 400m

As of 31st December 1990

MALE 44.40 or better

43.29	Butch Reynolds	USA	1988
43.86A	Lee Evans	USA	1968
43.87	Steve Lewis	USA	1988
43.97A	Larry James	USA	1968
43.98	Danny Everett	USA	1988
44.14	Roberto Hernandez	CUB	1990
44.17	Innocent Egbunike	NGR	1987
44.21	Michael Johnson	USA	1990
44.26	Alberto Juantorena	CUB	1976
44.27	Alonso Babers	USA	1984
44.27	Antonio Pettigrew	USA	1989
44.30	Gabriel Tiacoh	CIV	1986
44.33	Thomas Schoenlebe	GDR	1987
44.35	Andrew Valmon	USA	1990
44.38	Darren Clark	AUS	1988
44.40	Fred Newhouse	USA	1976

FEMALE 49.50 or better

47.60	Marita Koch	GDR	1985
47.99	Jarmila Kratochvilova	TCH	1983
48.27	Olga Vladykina	URS	1985
48.59	Tatyana Kocembova	TCH	1983
48.83	Valerie Brisco-Hooks	USA	1984
49.05	Chandra Cheeseborough	USA	1984
49.11	Olga Nazarova	URS	1988
49.19	Maria Pinigina	URS	1983
49.24	Sabine Busch	GDR	1984
49.28	Irena Szewinska	POL	1976
49.30	Petra Muller	GDR	1988
49.43	Kathy Cook	GBR	1984
49.47	Aelita Yurchenko	URS	1988
49.50	Grit Breuer	GDR	1990

A = Altitude performance

To date, less than 30 male athletes have run inside 44.75 secs and less than 30 female athletes inside 50.25 secs. The only U.K. female athlete presently represented here is Kathy Cook — 49.43 secs when winning the 1984 Olympic Bronze Medal; whilst David Jenkins at 44.93 secs in the A.A.U. (now T.A.C.) Championships of 1975, Derek Redmond at 44.50 in Rome, 1987, and Roger Black at 44.59 in winning the 1986 European Championship are the only U.K. athletes inside 45.00. There will surely be more from the present groundswell of exceptional British talent in this event.

U.K. athletes can consider themselves in an élite class when running inside 45.50 (men) or inside 51.50 (women) (Table 8).

TABLE 8

U.K. MEN 400m			U.K. WOMEN 400m		
Derek Redmond	44.50	1987	Kathy Cook	49.43	1984
Roger Black	44.59	1986	Michelle Scutt	50.63	1982
David Jenkins	44.93	1975	Joslyn Hoyte-Smith	50.75	1982
Kriss Akabusi	44.93	1988	Linda Keough	51.09	1989
Brian Whittle	45.22	1988	Linsey Macdonald	51.16	1980
Phil Brown	45.26	1985	Donna Hartley	51.28	1975
Todd Bennett	45.27	1988			
Glen Cohen	45.49	1978			

However, the international scene is going through a very rapid rate of change in the women's event and it will not be long before the 51.50 secs standard will shift to 51.00.

Table 9 represents the U.K. 1st, 3rd, 6th and 10th performance each year since 1980. It gives some indication not only of the relative improvement of performance in the U.K., but also of the standards required of athletes to move into the U.K. National "pool".

TABLE 9
U.K. PERFORMANCE 400m

MEN

U.K. Ranking	1980	1981	1982	1983	1984	1985	1986	1987	1988	1989	1990
1	45.29	45.86	45.45	45.58	45.43	44.82	44.59	44.50	44.67	45.54	44.91
3	45.81	46.25	45.89	46.10	45.76	45.35	45.29	45.63	45.22	46.22	46.06
6	46.18	46.83	46.50	46.43	46.32	45.67	45.65	45.99	46.02	46.26	46.33
10	46.56	47.03	46.80	46.97	46.85	46.60	46.39	46.37	46.43	46.59	46.72

WOMEN

U.K. Ranking	1980	1981	1982	1983	1984	1985	1986	1987	1988	1989	1990
1	50.88	51.08	50.46	50.95	49.42	51.36	51.88	52.74	51.65	51.09	51.20
3	51.62	51.93	50.75	52.25	51.93	52.82	53.00	53.01	52.26	52.04	52.78
6	53.02	52.50	52.80	52.90	52.67	53.33	53.32	53.49	53.05	53.41	53.25
10	53.90	53.76	53.24	53.40	53.46	53.70	53.70	53.68	53.57	53.73	54.05

A performance of 47.50 (men) and 55.00 (women) will usually afford a U.K. athlete top 20 status; whilst a performance of 49.00 (junior men) and 56.00 (European junior women) or 57.00 (intermediate women) is a reasonable indication that an athlete is moving in the right direction for serious 400m/800m ambitions as a senior. Although there will be the occasional exception, it is doubtful that 400m performance at an earlier age is a realistic guide to future potential in this event. More probable is that it could be a pointer to a sound base for middle distance development.

The young sprinter should not run 400's if he sees the event as middle distance! As a rule of thumb, athletes should be running 200m inside 25.00 (male) and 28.00 (female) before 400m is given serious consideration for specific development. Against this backcloth, the event will merit the athlete's concentrated attention once times of 54 secs (male) and 60 secs (female) are achieved without *too* much discomfort. The coach might well consider the most critical pointers for 400m as — Good performance over 100m, or over a rolling 30m/60m; plus capacity to concentrate and be competitive for up to a minute; plus commitment to the extra work loads and discomfort the shorter distance athletes do not require in such great measure.

The point must be made that at root the 400m and 200m athletes *must* have sprinting ability. Not every athlete will display this as a performance over 100m from blocks. — but all will certainly display quality over 30m or 60m from a rolling start. Good 200m and 400m athletes are *not* failed 100m athletes!

The event is started from a crouch start, using blocks. Although *the start* sees the athlete using a *driving* stride over the first 20m-30m, the "explosive" nature of the driving action is not as for 100m or 200m. It is too costly in energy terms to do so. Rather, the athlete looks to get into his pace for one lap as quickly but as economically as possible. In some ways, then, virtually all of the first bend (100m) is *the start*. The drive must then quickly shift to the striding technique as described for the middle portion of the 100m. Coming out of the first bend the athlete moves into the "meat" of the race, which is the 200m stretch from 100m to 300m.

It is important to establish this as a concept for athletes. Without doubt the athlete's performance over the "middle 200m" is the key to the eventual result. The sprinting technique is essentially "striding". Of course, the athlete will, depending on circumstances, mix *striding* and *lifting* in this phase; he may attempt the technique of working to accelerate into and out of bends, sometimes referred to as "burns"; he may also aim for a target half way time at 200m; but whatever, the 100m-300m section *must* be controlled carefully as a unit and must be worked on in terms of fitness and technique. The event must not be viewed as a flat out 200m followed by 200m of hanging on! The run off the final bend, and the final straight itself, is a continuation of the striding action. The 400m athlete in reacting to pressure from opponents for increased pace, should work on *lifting* if this occurs over the first 200m-300m of the race. However, this will only apply when the athlete *knows* that the pace of his own running is down relative to his own 400m optimum. If he *is* running at optimum 400m pace — he must not even think of reacting! *Control in maintaining form* in striding is the key coaching point.

When the pressure comes in the home straight, the athlete must work to maintain control and effectiveness of the striding action. Fatigue is obviously making its presence felt and this, amongst other things, is manifest in a slower rate of striding. The foot is, therefore, in contact longer with the track. The athlete should not attempt to return to something like a driving action, prolonging contact even more! Rather, lightness without loss of range of striding action with concentration on maintaining the sprinting rhythm are the key coaching points.

2.40   4 × 100m

The "sprint relay" has progressed a long way from being a "postscript" event for sprinters, long jumpers, hurdlers and so on at the end of an athletics meeting. At international level, it has become every bit as specialised as the individual events. This has happened for three main reasons:

— In events such as the Europa Cup and the athletics league competitions, relay success is as important as individual success in contribution to team points and, therefore, to establishing the Nation's international status and the club's status respectively.

— Athletes and coaches have greater appreciation of the value of a relay medal in the Major Championships.

— Commitment to training and competition in preparation for major championships, coupled with greater acceptance of being part of a team in a sport which is essentially "individual oriented", can produce relay success over teams which, on paper, are far superior in sprinting ability. Examples of this are — Czechoslovakia — European Champions in

1971 — without an athlete in the individual sprint finals; Scotland — Commonwealth Games Champions in 1978 with only Allan Wells reaching semi-final/final level in the individual 100 & 200; Nigeria — Commonwealth Champions in 1982 — who had no finalists in 100m or 200m; and USSR, Olympic Champions in 1988, who likewise had no individual sprint finalists.

This said, clearly there is correlation between relay performance and the quality of sprinters in the team. The athletes *must* have established sprinting ability, and be capable of blending this ability through personal discipline and relevant additional techniques, to the corporate demands of a team. The "team", in this instance, is normally a total of 7-9 persons, including the coach, who stresses that the quality of the "starting 4" depends on the quality of the "support 2-4".

The "barrier" separating the "super élite team" from the "mere mortals" is 38.00 secs for men (average per 100m relay leg = 9.50 secs) and 41.80 secs for women (average per 100m relay leg = 10.45 secs). Table 10 illustrates just how élite this club is.

The object of the event is to move the relay baton as fast as possible over 400m. This, in effect, means:

1. That each of the four athletes must cover their respective relay legs as fast as their sprinting ability will permit;

2. That loss of baton speed in transferring the baton from one athlete to the next must be avoided. The sprinting technique for each athlete is as for the individual 100m. Each athlete *drives* from a crouch position, the first athlete using blocks.

In pursuit of (1), techniques of *striding* and *lifting* are afforded ample opportunity for rehearsal in relay legs. In fact, relays are probably the best technical bridge from training to competition at the start of the season.

In pursuit of (2) the transfer of the baton (exchange) must take place in the 20m zone, at a point when the speed of incoming athlete (giving the baton) and outgoing athlete (receiving the baton) are matched. This means that the outgoing athlete starts his run when the athlete carrying the baton reaches a pre-arranged "check mark" which the outgoing athlete has measured out and placed on the track. The techniques of baton exchange, and selection of athletes for specific legs, will be discussed in greater detail later. Suffice it to say at this juncture, that the concept of the baton being exchanged "on the move" as a result of reaction to a visual cue to ensure no loss of baton speed is of rather more fundamental import. This, coupled with consistency of quality sprinting over the legs themselves, provides the foundation on which consideration of exchange techniques is built.

TABLE 10

MEN 4 × 100m — 38.00 or better

37.79	FRA	1990 — Moriniere	Sangouma	Trouabal	Marie Rose
37.83	USA	1984 — Graddy	Brown	Smith	Lewis
37.86	USA	1983 — King	Gault	Smith	Lewis
37.90	USA	1987 — McRae	McNeill	Glance	Lewis
37.93	USA*	1990 — Witherspoon	Burrell	Heard	Lewis
37.98	USA	1985 — McRae	Heard	Glance	Lewis
37.98	GBR	1990 — Braithwaite	Regis	Adam	Christie

* Actually Santa Monica Track Club

WOMEN 4 × 100m — 41.80 or better

41.37	GDR	1985 — Gladisch	Rieger	Auerswald	Gohr
41.53	GDR	1983 — Gladisch	Koch	Auerswald	Gohr
41.55	USA	1987 — Brown	Williams	Griffith	Marshall
41.58	USA	1987 — Brown	Williams	Griffith	Marshall
41.60	GDR	1980 — Muller	Wockel	Auerswald	Gohr
41.61	USA	1982 — Brown	Williams	Cheeseborough	Ashford
41.63	USA	1983 — Brown	Williams	Cheeseborough	Ashford
41.65	USA	1984 — Brown	Bolden	Cheeseborough	Ashford
41.65	GDR	1985 — Gladisch	Koch	Auerswald	Gohr
41.68	GDR	1990 — Gladisch	Krabbe	Behrendt	Guenther
41.69	GDR	1984 — Gladisch	Koch	Auerswald	Gohr
41.73	GDR	1988 — Gladisch	Behrendt	Auerswald	Gohr
41.76	GDR	1983 — Gladisch	Koch	Auerswald	Gohr
41.79	GDR	1987 — Gladisch	Drechsler	Auerswald	Gohr

Gladisch later Moller; Griffith later Griffith-Joyner; Auerswald later Lange.

The event must be seen both by athletes and coach as a team event. Four athletes win the medal; not just the best sprinter in the squad — and not just the man who runs the final leg! This implies commitment of time to working with colleagues in practice sessions and consequently requires, from time to time, rearrangement of personal training programmes. Such commitment is worthless, however, if such rearrangement compromises development of individual sprinting ability. The individual must not lose those qualities and competitive edge which have made him eligible for the relay team in the first place! The balance of individual programme v team training is not, then, an easy one to establish, and the relay coach must think on his feet to find that balance, leaning heavily on man-management skills. If, despite such efforts, the coach concludes that an individual athlete is unable to meet the demands of personal programme and requirements of being in the Team, it is better for Team and individual that he is excluded.

Relay athletes consider ideal conditions to be dry, windless and warm. They do not like lane one nor lane eight. The receiving athletes like to be first on the move!

The exceptional level of performance these statistics represent is well illustrated by the fact that only eight national teams have run faster than 38.40 (men) and seven faster than 42.70 (women) (Table 11).

TABLE 11 (4 × 100m)

MEN 38.40 — National teams			WOMEN 42.70 — National teams		
37.79	FRA	1990	41.37	GDR	1985
37.83	USA	1984	41.55	USA	1987
37.98	GBR	1990	42.00	URS	1980
38.02	URS	1987	42.31	BUL	1987
38.29	GDR	1982	42.43	GBR	1980
38.33	POL	1980	42.59	FRG	1976
38.37	ITA	1983	42.68	FRA	1982
38.39A	JAM	1968			

U.K. National teams can be considered as outstanding once they are inside 38.70 (men) and 43.00 (women) (Table 12). Targets for our European Junior Age Group are also included.

TABLE 12

MEN — UK 4 × 100m 38.70 or better

37.98	1990	—	Braithwaite	Regis	Adam	Christie
38.28	1988	—	Bunney	Regis	McFarlane	Christie
38.34	1989	—	Callender	Regis	Adam	Christie
38.39	1989	—	Jarrett	Regis	Adam	Christie
38.52	1988	—	Bunney	Regis	McFarlane	Christie
38.62	1980	—	McFarlane	Wells	Sharp	McMaster
38.67	1990	—	Callender	Regis	Adam	Christie
38.68	1984	—	Thompson	Reid	McFarlane	Wells

National European Junior Team Target is sub 40.00.

National Junior Record (as at 31st December 1990)

39.78	1990	—	Livingston	Smith	Williams	John

WOMEN — UK 4 × 100m 43.00 or better

42.43	1980	—	Oakes	Cook	Callender	Lannaman
42.66	1982	—	Hoyte	Cook	Callender	Thomas
42.71	1983	—	Baptiste	Cook	Callender	Thomas
42.72	1978	—	Callender	Cook	Danville	Lannaman

National European Junior Team Target is sub 45.00.

National Junior Record (as at 31st December 1990)

44.16	1990	—	Soper	Smith	Fraser	Merry

At club level, whilst there are often difficulties in keeping together a squad, let alone a team, Table 13 affords a guide to those performances which will enable a team to be competitive in most inter-club meets.

TABLE 13

	SENIOR	EURO JUNIOR	YOUTH/INTERMEDIATE
Men	42.00	43.60	44.40
Women	47.00	48.60	49.40

2.50 4 × 400

Formerly referred to in English speaking journals in the days of 440 yard tracks as ''the mile relay'', this event is enjoying an elevation of status similar to that of the 4 × 100m. It remains the case that a team may produce a world class performance yet not have all athletes as 400m specialists. For example, the British team which ran a European record in 1990 consisted of 2 × 400m specialists, 1 × 200m specialist and 1 × 100m Hurdles specialist! However, without doubt, the future of the event will be decided by those who can commit as a team of outstanding 4 × 400m relay athletes! The reasons for the ''elevation of status'' are similar to those listed for 4 × 100m — but, in addition, 4 × 400 has always enjoyed the spotlight of being ''the final event'' in most athletic programmes. With competitions from league inter-club to internationals often ''hanging'' on the 4 × 400, greater emphasis has been placed on ensuring quality of team member; strategic location of athletes in the running order; patterns of running each leg; and tactical sophistication of the ''anchor leg'' (final leg) athlete.

At first sight it would appear that there is less importance attached to loss of baton speed during baton exchange compared with the 4 × 100m. However, at the highest level, there can be little doubt that finesse is required even if the fine focus of check marks etc., is not involved. As for the one lap relay, the concept of ''a team'' applies, with athletes selected for their capacity to blend their talents within the four part unit as much as for their basic performance over 400m.

In this event the performance which determines the ''super-élite'' is sub 3 mins for men, and sub 3 mins 20.00 secs. for women. The leading performances as at 31st December 1990 are listed in Table 14.

TABLE 14

MEN 4 × 400m 3:00.00 or better

2:56.16A	USA	1968	Matthews	Freeman	James	Evans
2:56.16	USA	1988	Everett	Lewis	Robinzine	Reynolds
2:57.29	USA	1987	Everett	Haley	McKay	Reynolds
2:57.91	USA	1984	Nix	Armstead	Babers	McKay
2:58.22	GBR	1990	Sanders	Akabusi	Regis	Black
2:58.65	USA	1976	Frazier	Brown	Newhouse	Parks
2:58.86	GBR	1987	Redmond	Akabusi	Black	Brown
2:59.06	USA	1987	Everett	Franks	Pierre	McKay
2:59.12	USA	1981	McCoy	Wiley	Smith	Darden
2:59.13	GBR	1984	Akabusi	Cook	Bennett	Brown
2:59.16	CUB	1987	Penalver	Pavo	Martinez	Hernandez
2:59.32	NGR	1984	Uti	Ugbisie	Peters	Egbunike

2:59.52	USA	1976	Frazier	Brown	Newhouse	Parks
2:59.54	USA	1987	Rowe	Robinzine	Pierre	Haley
2:59.54	USA	1990	Daniel	Pettigrew	Valmon	Simon
2:59.6	USA	1966	Frey	Evans	Smith	Lewis
2:59.64A	KEN	1968	Asati	Nyamau	Bon	Rudisha
2:59.7	AUS	1984	Frayne	Clark	Minihan	Mitchell
2:59.71A	CUB	1988	Martinez	Valentin	Stevens	Hernandez
2:59.72	CUB	1987	Penalver	Pavo	Martinez	Hernandez
2:59.83	KEN	1972	Asati	Nyamau	Ouko	Sang
2:59.84	GBR	1986	Redmond	Akabusi	Whittle	Black
2:59.84	USA	1987	McCoy	Robinzine	Pierre	Haley
2:59.86	GDR	1985	Moller	Schersing	Carlowitz	Schoenlebe
2:59.86	USA	1987	Franks	Simon	Lowery	Nix
2:59.91A	USA	1983	Brown	Brooks	Rolle	McCoy
2:59.91	USA	1988	Lewis	Young	Everett	Thomas
2:59.96	FRG	1987	Dobeleit	Henrich	Itt	Schmid

WOMEN 4 × 400m 3:20.00 or better

3:15.17	URS	1988	Ledovskaya	Nazarova, O.	Pinigina	Bryzgina
3:15.51	USA	1988	Howard, D.	Dixon	Brisco	Griffith-Joyner
3:15.92	GDR	1984	Walther	Busch	Rubsam	Koch
3:16.87	GDR	1986	Emmelmann	Busch	Muller	Koch
3:18.29	USA	1984	Leatherwood	Howard, S.	Brisco	Cheeseborough
3:18.29	GDR	1988	Neubauer	Emmelmann	Busch	Muller
3:18.58	URS	1985	Nazarova, I.	Olizarenko	Pinigina	Vladykina
3:18.63	GDR	1987	Neubauer	Emmelmann	Muller	Busch
3:19.04	GDR	1982	Siemon	Busch	Rubsam	Koch
3:19.12	URS	1984	Baskakova	Nazarova, I.	Pinigina	Vladykina
3:19.23	GDR	1976	Maletzki	Rohde	Streidt	Brehmer
3:19.49	GDR	1985	Emmelmann	Busch	Neubauer	Koch
3:19.5	URS	1987	Yurchenko	Nazarova, O.	Pinigina	Bryzgina
3:19.6	USA	1984	Leatherwood	Howard, S.	Brisco	Cheeseborough
3:19.62	GDR	1979	Kotte	Brehmer	Kohn	Koch
3:19.66	GDR	1988	Losch	Emmelmann	Neubauer	Muller
3:19.73	GDR	1983	Walther	Busch	Koch	Rubsam
3:19.83	GDR	1981	Rubsam	Steuk	Wockel	Koch

Rubsam later Neubauer; Brisco formerly Brisco-Hooks; Siemon later Emmelmann; Muller now Schersing.

The exceptional level of performance represented by the women's statistics is well illustrated by the fact that only 9 national teams have run faster than 3:25.00 (Table 15). As for the men's statistics, it should be pointed out that until 1984 only two national teams had run under 3:00.00 mins.

TABLE 15

WOMEN — National teams 4 × 400m

3:15.17	URS	1988	Ledovskaya	Nazarova, O.	Pinigina	Bryzgina
3:15.51	USA	1988	Howard, D.	Dixon	Brisco	Griffith-Joyner
3:15.92	GDR	1984	Walther	Busch	Rubsam	Koch
3:20.32	TCH	1983	Kocembova	Moravcikova	Matejko-vicova	Kratochvilova
3:21.21	CAN	1984	Crooks	Richardson	Killingbeck	Payne
3:22.49	FRG	1988	Thimm	Arendt	Thomas	Abt
3:23.13	JAM	1988	Richards	Thomas	Rattray	Powell
3:24.65	POL	1986	Kasprzyk	Wojdecka	Kapusta	Blaszak
3:24.78	GBR	1990	Gunnell	Stoute	Beckford	Keough

U.K. National Teams can be considered as outstanding once they are inside 3:01.50 (men) and 3:27.00 (women) (Table 16).

TABLE 16

MEN — UK 4 × 400m 3:01.50 or better

2:58.22	1990	Sanders	Akabusi	Regis	Black
2:58.86	1987	Redmond	Akabusi	Black	Brown
2:59.13	1984	Akabusi	Cook	Bennett	Brown
2:59.84	1986	Redmond	Akabusi	Whittle	Black
3:00.46	1972	Reynolds	Pascoe	Hemery	Jenkins
3:00.68	1982	Jenkins	Cook	Bennett T.	Brown
3:01.12	1987	Harmsworth	Whittle	Bennett T.	Black
3:01.21A	1968	Winbolt-Lewis	Campbell	Hemery	Sherwood
3:01.26	1972	Reynolds	Pascoe	Hemery	Jenkins
3:01.47	1987	Thomas	Akabusi	Bennett T.	Brown

National European Junior Team Target is sub 3.06.00.

National Junior Record (as at 31st December 1990)

3:03.80	1990	Grindley	Patrick	Winrow	Richardson

WOMEN — UK 4 × 400m 3:27.00 or better

3:24.78	1990	Gunnell	Stoute	Beckford	Keough
3:25.51	1984	Scutt	Barnett	Taylor	Hoyte-Smith
3:25.82	1982	Cook	Macdonald	Taylor	Hoyte-Smith
3:25.87	1982	Forsyth	Hoyte-Smith	Elder	Scutt
3:26.54	1989	Keough	Stoute	Piggford	Gunnell
3:26.6	1975	Roscoe	Taylor	Elder	Hartley
3:26.89	1988	Keough	Stoute	Piggford	Gunnell

National European Junior Team Target is sub 3.37.00.

National Junior Record (as at 31st December 1990)

3:35.10	1985	Honley	Robinson	Flockhart	Hall

At club level, the following gives some guide to what will be a competitive performance in most inter-club competitions (Table 17).

TABLE 17

	SENIOR	EURO JUNIOR	YOUTH/ INTERMEDIATE
Men	3:16.00	3:28.00	3:36.00
Women	3:46.00	3:52.00	—

The U.K. Olympic and World Championships Team in men's 4 × 400m has an excellent record (Table 18).

TABLE 18

1912	Bronze	3:23.20	Nicol	Henley	Soutter	Seedhouse
1920	Gold	3:22.20	Griffiths	Lindsay	Ainsworth-Davies	Butler
1924	Bronze	3:17.40	Toms	Renwick	Ridley	Butler
1932	Silver	3:11.20	Stoneley	Hampson	Burghley	Rampling
1936	Gold	3:09.00	Wolff	Rampling	Roberts	Brown
1956	Bronze	3:07.20	Salisbury	Wheeler	Higgins	Johnson
1964	Silver	3:01.60	Graham	Metcalfe	Cooper	Brightwell
1972	Silver	3:00.46	Reynolds	Pascoe	Hemery	Jenkins
1983	Bronze	3:03.53	Bennett, A.	Cook	Bennett, T.	Brown
1984	Silver	2:59.13	Akabusi	Cook	Bennett T.	Brown
1987	Silver	2:58.86	Redmond	Akabusi	Black	Brown

This "tradition" has afforded athletes and coaches valuable education through experience of the event. The first three athletes have the job of producing maximum performance 400m so that the final athlete is put in a position to apply what tactics and strengths are necessary to achieve success. The first athlete is probably the only athlete who views his leg as being close to the individual event. He *drives* from a crouch start using blocks and is in lanes for the first lap. The stagger (distance between the starting lines for different lanes) is greater than for the individual event, because the second athlete *also* remains in lane for one bend. The second athlete like the third and fourth, takes the baton on the move from an upright start, within a 20m exchange zone. There is no acceleration zone for 4 × 400m. The *driving* phase is not as marked, then, as for the first athlete. The second athlete is first to be involved in what is potentially a "contact" event. He must have the ability to vary technique between drive, stride and lift, in pursuit of his contribution to the overall result. Running in balance; being able to move in or out to avoid physical contact; judging personal and opposition pace; and so on — are all parts of this athlete's armoury — and that of the third and fourth athlete. The third and fourth athletes have the problem of physical contact in the take over zone. Each must endeavour to make himself clearly visible to the incoming runner; to create a "window" in the line of athletes waiting to take the incoming athlete's baton; to afford space for the baton exchange to take place; and to take the baton on the move. The third athlete must have all the attributes of the second and represents the final opportunity for the last athlete to be put in a competitive position. The last athlete should be the *only* athlete who applies tactics geared to the simple objective of beating the opposition.

3.00 CONDITIONS FOR IMPROVING PERFORMANCE

The most depressing piece of coaching "news" I ever heard was that "Sprinters are born — not made". The postcript to this piece of pessimism was that "the contractile speed of a muscle fibre cannot be increased in one's lifetime". At a stroke, the nature v nurture argument could be declared "no contest". After all, if the limits were set at birth, we were clutching at straws to believe that technique, strength, mobility and endurance development could collectively compensate for an athlete's parental handicap! In short, such comments, if accepted at face value, can make of coaching a worthless pursuit!

The fact is that, of course, there are athletes who are more naturally gifted than others, but giftedness is no guarantee of competitive superiority. Moreover, no matter how fast an athlete can run when be begins a training programme, he will be able to run faster when the programme has been followed through. Life in general, and coaching in particular, is not about resigning ourselves to limits. It is about looking beyond present standards; of aiming for an improved condition, of believing that today's medal or record was good but not perfection and that tomorrow's will bring us a little closer.

It cannot be put down to happy parental coincidence that sprinters are getting faster (see tables 3, 6, 9) and will continue to do so. (Table 19).

TABLE 19

Projected World Records

	1980		1984		1988		1992		1996	
100	9.95a	10.88	9.93a	10.76	9.92	10.49	9.86	10.49	9.86	10.49
200	19.72a	21.71	19.72a	21.71	19.72a	21.34	19.72	21.34	19.70	21.34
400	43.86a	48.60	43.86a	47.99	43.29	47.60	43.29	47.60	43.15	47.60
4 × 100	38.03	41.60	37.83	41.53	37.83	41.30	37.75	41.25	36.69	41.20
4 × 400	2:56.16a	3:19.20	2:56.16a	3:15.92	2:56.16	3:15.17	2:55.15	3:14.80	2:54.65	3:14.45

1980 and 1988 are the world records at the end of these years. 1992 and 1996 are based on predictions by Bauersfeld (1977), Khomenkov (1979), averaged and adjusted by Dick (1990) in light of 1977-1990 progressions. The 1977 and 1979 work for men's 100, 200, 400 and 4 × 400 were based on altitude criteria.

The conditions required for improvement to continue, might be embraced under 7 broad headings.

1. *Coaches and athletes must believe that the athletes can be coached to sprint faster.* This belief can only grow where coaches base their work on sound interpretation of current training theory and coaching practice, and where there is clear evidence that the group, club, country, etc., can produce success. An example of the latter is surely the triggering of rapid growth in U.K. men's sprinting following the success of Allan Wells in 1978 and in 1980.

   A coach who does not believe in himself cannot expect athletes to believe in *him!* In accepting the responsibility of directing an athlete's athletic ambition, the coach must believe himself capable of doing so. The coaches' education programme will, of course, provide the coach with a sound basis for that belief. Through the programme he will have acquired information on structure and content of fail-safe training plans that are known to work. He will constantly seek advice in modifying such plans to meet the athletes specific needs. He will establish "credentials" in the shape of successful athletes coached, and as successive successful seasons unfold, experience will grow in parallel with continuing pursuit of knowledge to establish that level of expertise which will maintain the U.K.'s present excellent record in the sprints events.

2. *Young sprinters must be selected and coached well by coaches who have sound perspective on short, medium and long term objectives.* It takes time to produce real sprinting success.

   Coaches and athletes should view the junior years as part of long term development. This is not to say, however, that there are no immediate or short term objectives. Good coaching will always ensure that these are several and varied. This is part of creating the right "climate of motivation".

   The climate might include:—

   Achievement in control tests e.g. 30m flying; 60m blocks.....

   Competitive training targets e.g. "maximum competition" — max. press ups in 60 secs.

   Competition performance e.g. Personal bests in 60m, 100m,.....

   Competition results e.g. Championships, relays, etc.....

   Representative honours e.g. Club, Area, National Vests..... and so on.

   No athlete must ever feel that he's arrived, but he needs constant assurance that he's getting there!

3. *Coaches must understand technique, training and tactics* as they apply to one-off and tournament situations, as much as to the one and multiple year programmes. The chapters which follow may contribute to such understanding.

4. *Preparation and coaching methods and practices must look to innovation and variety whilst having inbuilt routine and system.* The content of this booklet, whilst offering suggestions, should also encourage coaches to exercise imagination in designing programmes.

5. *Training theory must be better applied to progression at the 1-4 year level, and at the special competition preparation level.* The role and application of support systems must also be understood and accepted as part of planning.

6. *There must be more appropriate competition progression gradients followed.* This is possible mainly through access to a greater number of relevant competition opportunities. The season's competition profile must, however, be carefully thought out before selecting and locating competitions within the annual calendar.

7. *Facilities and equipment provision more suited to sprint development must be pursued.* It is beyond the scope of this booklet to expand this heading. Suffice it to say that sprinters need warm and dry conditions, especially for technique, speed and high intensity work. Adequate indoor provision and access to warm-weather camps are, therefore, important in the sprinter's development.

4.00 CONTROL TESTS IN SELECTION AND DEVELOPMENT

Coaches do not normally adhere to a hard and fast universal criterion for selection. Seeing "raw" talent tells you very little. The athlete must be exposed to the discipline of training and competition before any real evaluation of potential can be established. Standard talent selection procedures are only applicable if preceded by standard training. This is only acceptable or possible in a totalitarian state. It seems sensible, then, to put the young sprinter through a control test battery at commencement and at conclusion of a training period — 3 months; 6 months; 1 year and so on. When this information is viewed alongside the more subjective evaluations of coach/athlete/squad compatability, competitiveness etc., only then can a coach have any basis for evaluating all those things which are embraced by "potential".

Both talent and progress can be evaluated through judicious application of control tests. The following are offered as suggested controls, with data included on the understanding that it affords only the loosest of guides. Most relevant information gained in applying the controls is at the test — retest level on a given athlete, and each coach should establish predictive indices etc. for individual athletes rather than squads. For example, athlete A may be within the 10.49 — 10.56 100m range, given control results of 3.80s 30m blocks; 2.68s 30m flying and 6.56s 60m blocks. Athlete B, whilst matching athlete A to the 100th over 60m competition, may be as much as 0.15 sec adrift over 100m. Table 20 is related to 60m, 100m and 200m controls. At the top end there can be problems of inconsistency in 60m: 100m competition comparisons as the concept of indoor 60m specialization emerges. The controls may be used in many ways, but broadly they afford evaluation as follows:—

30m flying	—	Full flight technique efficiency; speed.
60m blocks	—	Starting ability; pick-up to full flight.
150m standing	—	Endurance for 100m. (alactic anaerobic/lactic anaerobic)
250m standing	—	Endurance for 200m. (lactic anaerobic/alactic anaerobic)

If an athlete's times are falling outside the ranges suggested, then a relevant compensating programme or adjustment to the training cycle is indicated. Table 21 is related to 400m controls, but includes a control for 200m athletes additional to those in table 20. Broadly speaking, they afford evaluation as follows:—

150m standing	—	basis of 400m speed — (see also 100/200m controls) (alactic anaerobic/lactic anaerobic)
300m standing	—	speed endurance (lactic anaerobic/alactic anaerobic)
600m standing	—	strength/general endurance

300m time minus (2 × 150m time)	—	speed endurance index. If athlete's index greater, and provided 150m is in line with training targets, then more speed endurance work indicated. (→ Lactic Anaerobic)
600m time minus (2 × 300m time)	—	strength/general endurance index. If athlete's index greater, and provided 300m is in line with training targets, then more strength and general endurance work indicated. (→ aerobic)

TABLE 20

CONTROLS FOR 100m/200m ATHLETES

Time Trials — hand timed.　　　　　　　　　　　Competition Performance.
　　　　　　　　　　　　　　　　　　　　　　　(electric timing)

30m from Blocks	30m Flying	60m from Blocks	150m from Standing*	250 from Standing*	60m	100m ϕ	200m
3.58-3.61	2.48-2.51	6.22-6.27	14.87-14.97	25.47-25.72	6.49-6.53	10.09-10.16	20.17-20.32
3.62-3.65	2.52-2.55	6.28-6.33	14.98-15.08	25.73-25.98	6.54-6.58	10.17-10.24	20.33-20.48
3.66-3.69	2.56-2.59	6.34-6.39	15.09-15.19	25.99-26.24	6.59-6.63	10.25-10.32	20.49-20.64
3.70-3.73	2.60-2.63	6.40-6.45	15.20-15.30	26.25-26.50	6.64-6.68	10.33-10.40	20.65-20.80
3.74-3.77	2.64-2.67	6.46-6.51	15.31-15.42	26.51-26.76	6.69-6.73	10.41-10.48	20.81-20.96
3.78-3.81	2.68-2.71	6.52-6.57	15.43-15.54	26.77-27.02	6.74-6.78	10.49-10.56	20.97-21.12
3.82-3.85	2.72-2.75	6.58-6.63	15.55-15.66	27.03-27.28	6.79-6.83	10.57-10.64	21.13-21.28
3.86-3.89	2.76-2.79	6.64-6.69	15.67-15.79	27.29-27.54	6.84-6.88	10.65-10.72	21.29-21.44
3.90-3.93	2.80-2.83	6.70-6.75	15.80-15.92	27.55-27.80	6.89-6.93	10.73-10.80	21.45-21.61
3.94-3.98	2.84-2.88	6.76-6.81	15.93-16.06	27.81-28.06	6.94-7.00	10.81-10.90	21.62-21.88
3.99-4.03	2.89-2.93	6.82-6.87	16.07-16.20	28.07-28.31	7.01-7.06	10.91-11.00	21.89-22.09
4.04-4.08	2.94-2.98	6.88-6.93	16.21-16.35	28.32-28.55	7.07-7.12	11.01-11.09	22.10-22.30
4.09-4.13	2.99-3.03	6.94-6.99	16.36-16.51	28.56-28.80	7.13-7.18	11.10-11.19	22.31-22.50
4.14-4.18	3.04-3.08	7.00-7.05	16.52-16.68	28.81-29.06	7.19-7.25	11.20-11.29	22.51-22.72
4.19-4.24	3.09-3.14	7.06-7.12	16.69-16.86	29.07-29.34	7.26-7.32	11.30-11.40	22.73-22.95
4.25-4.30	3.15-3.20	7.13-7.19	16.87-17.05	29.35-29.63	7.33-7.39	11.41-11.51	22.96-23.19
4.31-4.36	3.21-3.26	7.20-7.26	17.06-17.25	29.64-29.91	7.40-7.46	11.52-11.62	23.20-23.43
4.37-4.42	3.27-3.32	7.27-7.33	17.26-17.46	29.92-30.19	7.47-7.53	11.63-11.73	23.44-23.69
4.43-4.48	3.33-3.38	7.34-7.40	17.47-17.67	30.20-30.50	7.54-7.61	11.74-11.85	23.70-23.95
4.49-4.54	3.39-3.44	7.41-7.50	17.68-17.88	30.51-30.91	7.62-7.71	11.86-12.01	23.96-24.27
4.55-4.60	3.45-3.50	7.51-7.60	17.89-18.09	30.92-31.32	7.72-7.81	12.02-12.17	24.28-24.64
4.61-4.70	3.51-3.60	7.61-7.70	18.10-18.30	31.33-31.74	7.82-7.91	12.18-12.33	24.65-24.98
4.71-4.80	3.61-3.70	7.71-7.80	18.31-18.55	31.75-32.15	7.92-8.02	12.34-12.49	24.99-25.30
4.81-4.90	3.71-3.80	7.81-7.90	18.56-18.81	32.16-32.56	8.03-8.12	12.50-12.65	25.31-25.65
4.91-5.00	3.81-3.90	7.91-8.00	18.82-19.12	32.57-33.06	8.13-8.25	12.66-12.85	25.65-25.99
5.0-5.1	3.9-4.0	8.0-8.1	19.2-19.6	33.1-33.7	8.3-8.4	12.9-13.1	26.0-26.5
5.1-5.2	4.0-4.1	8.1-8.2	19.6-20.0	33.7-34.3	8.4-8.5	13.1-13.3	26.5-27.0
5.2-5.3	4.1-4.2	8.2-8.3	20.0-20.4	34.3-35.0	8.5-8.7	13.3-13.6	27.0-27.5
5.3-5.5	4.2-4.4	8.3-8.5	20.4-20.8	35.0-35.6	8.7-8.9	13.6-13.9	27.5-28.0

* Timed from first foot contact over start line.

ϕ Possible inconsistency where there are specialist 60m indoor athletes.

TABLE 21

CONTROLS FOR 400m AND ENDURANCE CONTROLS FOR 200m

Competition Performance	200m Endurance Control			400m Endurance Control		Competition Performance
200	150 from* Standing	300m from* Standing	300 – (2 × 150)	600 from* Standing	600 – (2 × 300)	400
20.3-20.4	14.9-15.0	31.7-31.9	1.9	71.2-71.7	7.8	43.9-44.0
20.4-20.5	15.0-15.1	32.0-32.1	1.9	71.8-72.1	7.9	44.1-44.2
20.5-20.6	15.1-15.2	32.2-32.3	1.9	72.2-72.6	7.9	44.3-44.5
20.6-20.7	15.2-15.3	32.4-32.6	2.0	72.7-73.2	8.0	44.6-44.9
20.7-20.8	15.3-15.4	32.7-32.8	2.0	73.3-73.8	8.0	45.0-45.2
20.8-20.9	15.4-15.5	32.9-33.0	2.0	73.9-74.4	8.1	45.3-45.5
20.9-21.0	15.5-15.6	33.1-33.3	2.1	74.5-75.0	8.2	45.6-45.9
21.0-21.1	15.6-15.7	33.4-33.6	2.2	75.1-75.7	8.3	46.0-46.3
21.1-21.3	15.7-15.8	33.7-33.9	2.3	75.8-76.4	8.4	46.4-46.7
21.3-21.4	15.8-15.9	34.0-34.2	2.4	76.5-77.1	8.5	46.8-47.1
21.4-21.6	15.9-16.0	34.3-34.5	2.5	77.2-77.9	8.6	47.2-47.6
21.6-21.8	16.0-16.1	34.6-34.8	2.6	78.0-78.7	8.7	47.7-48.0
21.8-21.9	16.1-16.2	34.9-35.1	2.7	78.8-79.5	8.8	48.1-48.4
21.9-22.1	16.2-16.4	35.2-35.6	2.8	79.6-80.3	8.9	48.5-48.9
22.1-22.3	16.4-16.6	35.7-36.1	2.9	80.4-81.1	9.0	49.0-49.3
22.3-22.5	16.6-16.7	36.2-36.4	3.0	81.2-82.0	9.1	49.4-49.9
22.5-22.7	16.7-16.9	36.5-36.9	3.1	82.1-82.9	9.2	50.0-50.6
22.7-22.9	16.9-17.0	37.0-37.2	3.2	83.0-83.9	9.3	50.7-51.2
22.9-23.1	17.0-17-2	37.3-27.7	3.3	84.0-85.0	9.4	51.3-51.8
23.1-23.3	17.2-17.3	37.8-38.0	3.4	85.1-86.2	9.5	51.9-52.4
23.3-23.6	17.3-17.5	38.1-38.6	3.6	86.3-87.4	9.6	52.5-53.1
23.6-23.9	17.5-17.7	38.7-39.1	3.7	87.5-88.6	9.8	53.2-53.9
23.9-24.2	17.7-17.9	39.2-39.6	3.8	88.7-89.8	10.0	54.0-54.6
24.2-24.5	17.9-18.0	39.7-39.9	3.9	89.9-91.0	10.2	54.7-55.3
24.5-24.8	18.0-18.3	40.0-40.5	4.0	91.1-92.2	10.4	55.4-56.0
24.8-25.1	18.3-18.6	40.6-41.2	4.2	92.3-93.5	10.6	56.1-56.8
25-1-25.5	18.6-18.8	41.3-41.9	4.3	93.6-94.8	10.8	56.9-57.6
25.5-25.8	18.8-19.0	42.0-42.5	4.4	94.9-96.1	11.0	57.7-58.5
25.8-26.1	19.0-19.3	42.6-43.1	4.5	96.2-97.4	11.2	58.6-59.4
26.1-26.5	19.3-19.6	43.2-43.9	4.6	97.5-99.0	11.4	59.5-60.5
26.5-27.0	19.6-20.0	44.0-44.8	4.8	99.1-101.2	11.6	60.6-61.8
27.0-27.5	20.0-20.4	44.9-45.7	4.9	101.3-103.2	11.8	61.9-63.0
27.5-28.0	20.4-20.8	45.8-46.6	5.0	103.3-105.2	12.0	63.1-64.2

* Timed from first foot contact over start line.

Note: The data here represents a loose guide linking control and competition performance. Athletes may produce a given performance in competition *without* meeting all control criteria! Tables must be adapted and interpreted by coach and athlete accordingly.

Coaches to 400m athletes should also use the sprint controls as occasion suggests, and in order to monitor sprinting speeds.

Table 22 is offered as a guide to specific leg strength. If athlete's scores are less than suggested, more general and special strength work is indicated.

TABLE 22

BOUNDING CONTROLS

Target Time	Standing Jump Long (m)	Reach (cm)	3 Bounds* (m)	5 Bounds* (m)	10 Bounds* (m)
10.20-10.65	2.90-3.20	76-85	9.20-10.00	15.90-17.10	29.50-39.50
10.70-11.10	2.70-3.00	68-77	8.50-9.10	14.60-15.60	27.00-37.00
11.20-11.70	2.60-2.90	60-69	7.90-8.50	14.00-15.00	25.00-35.00
11.80-12.20	2.50-2.80	53-61	7.50-8.10	13.40-14.40	23.00-33.00
12.30-12.70	2.40-2.70	46-54	7.20-7.80	12.80-13.80	21.00-31.00
12.80-13.20	2.30-2.60	39-47	6.80-7.40	12.20-13.20	19.00-29.00

* From standing.

Broad ranges reflect leg length variations as much as strength differences within groups. Coaches will establish tighter ranges for individual athletes and "height groups".

Note: The data here represents a loose guide linking control and competition performance. Athletes may produce a given performance in competition *without* meeting all control criteria! Tables must be adapted and interpreted by coach and athlete accordingly.

The controls listed are by no means exhaustive. They should be adapted, added to, or rejected in light of establishing a relevant personal test battery.

Finally, statistics at the bottom end of tables 20 and 21 — below the line — are presented as a guide for coaches working with athletes who are "fringing" the sprints group.

5.00 SPRINT TECHNIQUE

The general policy of development, be it with a beginner or élite athlete, is:—

(1) Establish basic fitness

(2) Establish basic technique

(3) Establish special fitness

(4) Establish advanced technique.

Within this framework, coaches work to build and refine technique only when the athlete is fit to learn it. Technique at no point must be compromised in pursuit of speed. Speed is seen as a sophistication of technique.

Technique

"Every runner, no matter whether he be a hundred metre specialist or a marathon man, is concerned with improving his horizontal speed. This is the product of the rate of striding and the length of stride."
(Bill Marlow — 'Sprinting and Relay Racing' — 1966)

Horizontal speed = stride length (metres) × stride rate (strides per second)

Because improvement in strength, mobility and technique can effect considerable increase in stride length, most early sprints coaching emphasised this aspect of the "equation" almost to the exclusion of any work on stride rate. The fact is that stride length *and* stride rate can be improved. Developments in speed assisted practices, such as downhill sprints, towing, elastic assist, and specific technique drills, have clearly indicated that this is the case.

Achieving an athlete's optimal product of stride length and stride rate is the result of expressing progressive development of physical and mental condition, through sound technique.

There are three clearly identifiable variants of basic sprinting technique.

(1) Sprint *stride* — The full flight striking action (Striding).

(2) Sprint *drive* — the starting action (Driving).

(3) Sprint *lift* — The "kick at speed" action (Lifting).

The coach should develop the athlete's sprinting technique in that order.

In technique training units, the coach should focus his attention on:—

POSTURE: The general impression of technique. Particular points are the position of head and trunk.

ARMS: The arm positions and actions.

LEGS: The leg positions and actions.

The coach observes and evaluates technique from three positions. (fig 1)

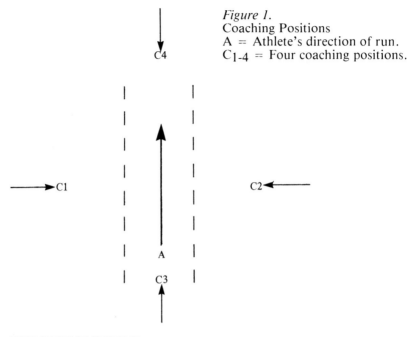

Figure 1.
Coaching Positions
A = Athlete's direction of run.
C_{1-4} = Four coaching positions.

5.10 THE SPRINT STRIDE

	(Figs — 2 Wells, 3 Gohr)
Posture:	The athlete has the appearance of "running tall".
	Shoulders are down, not hunched.
	There should be no signs of straining or tension on face and neck.
	There should be an impression of trunk "strength".
	There should be an impression of smooth, continuous motion as opposed to jerky, broken motion.
Arms: Men:	Approximately 90° angle at elbow is held.
	Full range of action is pursued — elbow pulled back and high with a strong "squeeze".
	Hand only comes to shoulder height in front.
Women:	Elbow angle as above — but elbows slightly out from the body.
	Short, fast "drum-beating" action — little of it behind the body.
Legs:	The athlete strikes the ground with a claw-like action from a high knee lift.
	A full range action is pursued.

Coaching Points

On a sound basis of strength, mobility and endurance, the coach observes the athlete over 60m. He works on posture, then arms, then legs, attempting to make essential adjustments to the athlete's basic striding technique as suggested by technical appraisal. The speed of run must be ½-¾ pace and never so fast that the developing technical model deteriorates.

Posture:		Athlete should "run tall", "feel strong" .....
		Shoulders should remain square to the front — no "rolling".....
		Eyes should look straight ahead.....
Arms:		Shoulders down..... "long neck".....
	Men:	Elbows squeezed high behind (figure 2.2)
		Hands only as far back as hip.....
		Hands only as high in front as shoulder (figure 2.9)
		Hands loosely clenched..... like holding something fragile.....
		Elbows brush vest.....
	Women:	Forearms beat fast down and back..... "drumming".....
		Hands only as high in front as breast level..... (figure 3.4)
		Hands only as far back as hip (figure 3.11)
		(Note: Compare end of Wells right arm action — Figure 2.2; and end of Gohr's right arm action — Figure 3.11) (Gohr's hands very floppy in beat-back).
		Hands loosely clenched.....
		Elbows — slightly out from vest — work for greater speed.....
Legs:		An athlete works on *early* development of stride-length; he must attempt to remain late in contact with the track..... "stay with the track....." ....."swing hip with thigh through full range....." etc. Once the feeling of range is established, the coach *then* builds in the striking/clawing action as a feeling of elastic bounce is brought into the movement.
		Knee lifted high enough to allow a striking/clawing action — (note: Wells' left leg action figure 2.2-12.) (note: Gohr's right leg action figure 3.3-16) "Don't push" — "strike!"..... "claw!".....

Much of the special strength work involving bounding, power runs, straight leg runs, "skip drills" and so on are geared not only to development of special strength, but of this variant of sprint technique by simulating the relevant joint actions and dynamics.

27

Figure 2.

Figure 3.

Competitions can be brought into technique training units for development of the sprint stride. For example:

— how far in 10 strides using striking action.
— how few strides in 30m. using striking action.
— etc.

5.20 THE SPRINT DRIVE

(Figs — 4 Quarrie, 5 Gohr, 6 Borzov)

Posture: The athlete is moving out of a start — "set" position, gradually opening from a "pike".

Back is initially rounded but flattens with the first strides.

There is a general impression of a horizontal thrust, with the body "low".

Eyes are down.

There should be minimal signs of effort on face and neck.

Arms: Men: The action is powerful through a very full range, reflecting the immense strength demands on the legs (figures 4 & 6). The range is, in fact, greater than in the *striding* technique, and should be emphasised. However, control is required to avoid a wild "flailing" in the pull back phase. The angle of approximately 90° at the elbow *must* be worked for. To ignore this technical problem will cause a slowing of the arm action at a time when the athlete requires their speed of action to lead a fast stride rate; can put the athlete off balance; and will cause unproductive trunk twisting.

Women: Dr. Karel Hoffman (Poland) established that a critical difference between male and female sprinters was stride rate. One interpretation of this and other supporting material, has been a deliberate attempt to improve the stride rate of female sprinters by concentrating on a faster arm action. In particular, this is applied to the driving phase of the sprint race.

The action is a reduced range very fast beating action, mainly in front of the body. (figure 5). It is fundamental, of course, that this arm action does not reduce efficacy of leg drive.

Legs: Very full range driving action. The athlete pushes the track behind him, with an exaggerated knee lift to the "piked" trunk.

Figure 4

Coaching Points

On a sound basis of strength, mobility and endurance, and with the athlete already conversant with the *striding* technique, the coach observes the athlete over 30m-40m. He works through posture, arms and legs as the athlete works from a semi, then full-crouch start without blocks. The latter are introduced once the driving technique is understood and reproducible. The speed of the run must be ½-¾ pace with the athlete in full control of technique.

Posture: Athlete should "stay low"..... "back strong and straight".....
Eyes should focus on the track.
Athlete should walk, jog etc., in "pike".....

Figure 5

Figure 6

Arms:		Arm action should be coached with athlete working to retain that used in *sprint stride.*
	Men:	Work on pulling elbow back to limit of range.
		"Let the arms do the running".....
		"Feel arms strong".....
	Women:	Work on effective range for the "beating" action
		"Feel arms light and fast"....
Legs:		The action is a pushing action.....
		"Feel *extension* — hip — knee — ankle".....
		"Pull knee to chest".....

Keep the athlete at a slow pace to feel the positions, balances, pushing action.

The athlete *must* have a sensation of *range,* extension, pushing, power.

Special strength work such as tyre pulling, hill running, etc., is not only geared to development of special strength, but also of this variant of sprint technique by simulating the "working" position and joint actions.

Again, competitions can be introduced into training units for development of the sprint drive. For example:

— how far in 10 strides using drive action
— how far in 10 strides pulling a tyre
— how few strides in 30m using drive action
— etc.

Clearly this technique is that applied at the start of a race. Once mastered, the athlete can work on his starting position.

5.30   THE START

The start of a sprint race is that part of the race from the athlete's reaction to the gun, in the "set" position, to the time he is in full flight. This incorporates:

> a set position
>
> a reaction to the gun
>
> a driving phase
>
> a striding phase.

It is a blended unit — not a series of separate bits!

It is preceded by the athlete assuming a crouched position on the instruction "on your marks". The athlete moves into the "set" position (starting position) in one movement. The athlete's starting position must enable him to react to the gun in such a way that he can execute an effective drive technique. This, in turn, will take the athlete smoothly into the striding phase.

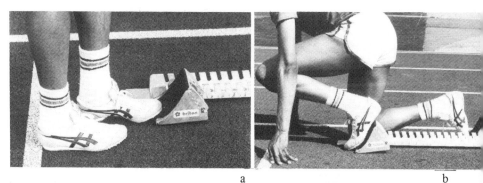

a   b

Figure 7

Coaching Points

No two athletes have identical starting positions. The coach should initiate the individual development process thus:—

(a)   Locate the athlete's foot position as per figure (7) to establish the "on your marks" position. This will allow movement into a set position very close to what has been described as the "medium start" by Franklin Henry.

(b)   Adjust hands and feet to a position *where the athlete feels comfortable,* and which in the set position approximates to:—

  i.   hands just wide of shoulder width apart, fingers and thumb affording a high bridge

  ii.   shoulders above to slightly ahead of hands

iii. arms straight but not "locked" at the elbow

iv. hips higher than shoulders

v. leading knee angle 90°

vi. Rear knee angle − 120°.

(see figures 8, 9, 10 for examples; and figure 11 for some idea of the variety of interpretation that can exist!)

(c) The action or rising into the set position must be one movement

(d) Instruct the athlete to run (not jump!) into the driving phase over 30m.

Figure 8 *Figure 9*

Figure 10

Figure 11

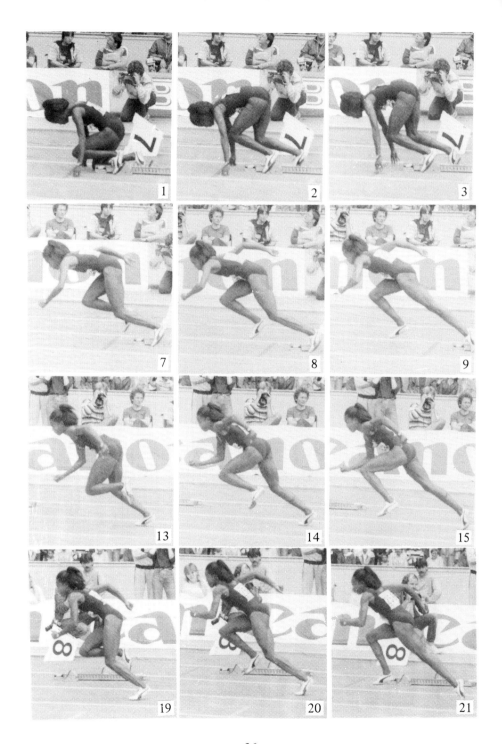

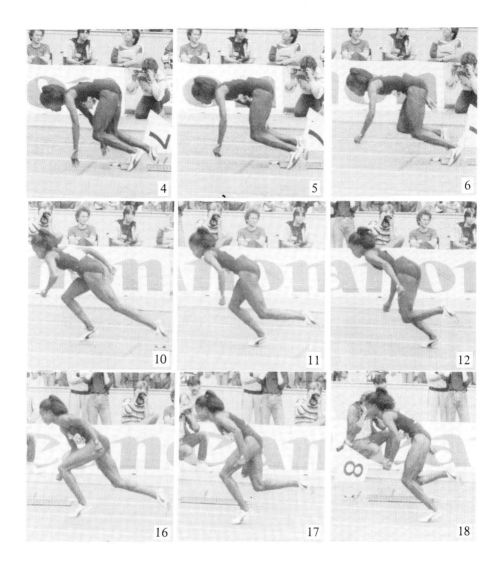

Figure 12

Much patience must be exercised in establishing the most appropriate start position for a given athlete. Once comfortable and effective, blocks can be introduced. They should be kept at a relatively flat angle to begin with, to allow the athlete to adapt to their presence (figure 13). Gradually the athlete will be sufficiently at home in using them to adjust the block angle to a more orthodox position. The athlete should by that time have with him whenever he is going to use blocks, a note of the distance of his front block from the line, and of his rear block from the front block. He should also know the block angles, and carry with him a small measuring tape. Investment in a set of personal blocks is worth while.

The concept of a driving, powerful start is captured by Ashford in Figure 12.

The point should be made here that there must be adjustment to the start when starting on the bend.

(1) The blocks should be angled to the starting line in such a way that they are at a tangent to the curve at its most distant point. (figure 14)

(2) The left hand must be withdrawn from the line.

The adjustment of the blocks is clearly seen in the frontal view of Quarrie (figure 15). The withdrawal of the left hand is illustrated in (figure 12,1 & 2).

The keys to good starting are:—

1. Concentrate on moving the *hands fast* in reaction to the gun.

2. *Keep low*..... (by placing an empty match box at each of the athlete's hands a useful coaching aid can be created. The athlete should knock the boxes away as he starts. If not, his shoulders have come up too early.)

3. *Run out*

An element of competition can be introduced to technical training units by operating the control test of driving at ½-¾ speed for 10 strides and measuring the distance covered.

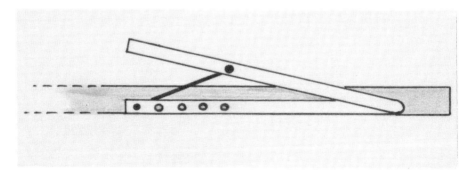

Figure 13
Flat square blocks

| Figure 14 | Figure 15 |

5.40 REACTIONS

The question is often asked — "can reaction time be improved?" Reaction, then, deserves some consideration here.

"Reaction" is frequently confused with "Reflex". They are not the same. Reaction is voluntary and therefore under the athlete's control. Reflexes are involuntary and, in taking place below the conscious level, are beyond the athlete's control.

The athlete seeks to react with appropriate coordinated joint actions and dynamics to a given signal: — the gun; or an incoming athlete reaching a relay checkmark; or the challenge of another athlete in competition.

The athlete is coached to learn such "appropriate coordination". Training, both technical and conditioning, helps establish the correct patterns of movement the athlete requires. Consequently the athlete reacts more efficiently through training. This in turn suggests that the athlete's central nervous system spends less time selecting the correct course of action to a signal! Current training theory also holds that reaction practices can improve reaction speed. Consequently, it can be said that reaction time *can* be improved. A footnote to this, however, is that speed of reactions is so well within the athlete's control, that he can vary it according to specific situation demands. For example, it is clear that reaction time in 100m is quicker than that of 200m which is, in turn, quicker than in 400m (Table 23).

TABLE 23

REACTION TIMES

DATA BASED ON WORLD CHAMPIONSHIPS 1983

		100m Semi Final 1	Semi Final 2	Final	200m Semi Final 1	Semi Final 2	Final	400m Semi Final 1	Semi Final 2	Final
Range of Reaction Times	Men	.125/.163	.121/.166	.125/.140	.164/.251	.142/.173	.161/.244	.204/.280	.161/.291	.165/.273
	Women	.130/.179	.146/.204	.131/.186	.167/.255	.175/.332	.161/.237	.192/.264	.202/.331	.171/.279

COMPARATIVE TIMES FOR INDIVIDUAL ATHLETES

100m	Round 1	Round 2	Semi Final	Final	200m	Round 1	Round 2	Semi Final	Final
Wells	.132	.131	.162	.125		.206	.161	.211	.213
Koch	.181	.162	.173	.172		.209	.208	.192	.225

5.50 THE SPRINT LIFT

(Figure 16)

Posture: The athlete has the appearance of "running tall' with a higher knee action than the stride technique.

Shoulders are down, not hunched.

There should be no signs of straining or tension on face and neck.

There should be an impression of lightness and speed.

Arms: The arm action is similar to that of the stride technique. The difference is slight increase in speed of action. The range is virtually the same, but for a more emphatic pumping/beating effect in front of the body.

The female action is actually a more exaggerated version of the emphasis in stride technique.

Legs: The leg action is characterised by a high lifting/prancing effect. It is a light, fast movement which is associated with a quicker, more active and lighter striking/clawing movement of the foot onto the track.

Figure 16

Coaching Points

This technique is normally only a feature of the experienced athlete's "armoury", but it can be introduced to the developing athlete's technique training programme. It is used when athletes require to "kick" whilst in full flight. Running off the bend in 200m; lifting for the tape in 100m; reacting to a challenge in 100m and 200m; these are occasions when the athlete may require to recruit this variant.

It requires a foundation of strength, mobility, endurance and mastery of the *stride* technique. The coach observes the athlete over 30m, following a rolling build up to ¾ speed. He works on posture — arms and legs in order shaping the *stride* technique towards the *lift* technique. Fatigue rather than speed will erode the technical model in this technique training unit, so small sets and full recoveries are important.

Posture:	Athlete should "run tall", "feel light".....
	Shoulders should remain square to the front..... "strong shoulders".....
	Chin should stay down, not out.....
Arms:	Shoulders down..... "long neck".....
Men:	"pumping/beating action" — "more urgency"..... "fast arms" — hands reach slightly above the shoulders.....
Women:	Faster beat with forearms..... "relaxed and light".....
Legs:	"lift knees"..... "prance"
	"Run on hot bricks"..... "Run on eggs".....
	"Fast and light....."

Again, much of the special strength work involving bounding, power runs, "skip drills", "lifting drills" and so on is geared both to specific conditioning and technique development.

5.60   RUNNING THE CURVE

Sprinters must be able to run straights and bends. (Figure 17) Once the athlete has developed a sound and stable version of a sprint technique

9   10   11   12

variant, working on the straight, he should then work occasionally on the bend, using different lanes from time to time.

Coaching Points

For beginner athletes, the centre circle on a soccer field is useful as a coaching aid. The coach should teach the athlete to:
— carry the left arm lower

— work full range with the right arm, but bring it across towards his chin

— work a natural leg action according to the various sprint technique requirements, whilst adjusting to the bend.
    An athlete drawing Lane 1 in 200m should run on the middle to outside of his lane. The extra distance cancels itself against the less severe bend radius. Other lanes should run close to but not on the line on the inside of the lane. Finally, the athlete must work to avoid letting himself drift to the outside of his lane as he comes off the bend into the straight.

Figure 17

6.00 RELAY TECHNIQUES

All sprinters will be required to run relays from time to time; and all sprint coaches will coach athletes in relay teams — or even coach a relay team or teams. It is important, then, that athletes and coaches understand relay techniques. However, it is equally important that athletes and coaches understand that the relays events are specialist events in their own right. They require strong individual and corporate commitment to achievement as a team through preparation as a team. Moreover, they require athletes and coaches to live the concept that the team comes before the individual. This, of course, is normally not the case in a sport which focuses mainly on individual achievement. But medals and points in relays are just as important to club and nation as are medals and points in individual events — and are just as hard to win!

6.10 4 × 100m (Figure 18)

This is a co-operative team event and achievement depends on the quality and quantity of team practices.

1. The starting ("lead-off") athlete must be a fast and reliable starter. He must also be a good bend runner. He carries the baton in his right hand and runs to the inside of his lane, even when in lane 1. He puts the baton into the left hand of the second ("back-straight") athlete in the first take-over zone. Because the "ideal" change-over will be executed approximately 5m from the end of the change-over zone, the first athlete will have run approximately 105m with the baton. (Figure 18)

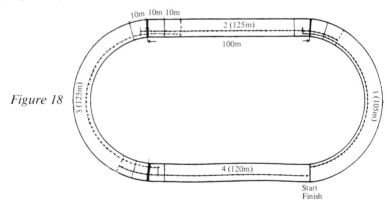

Figure 18

2. The second athlete must be a strong athlete — possible 200m specialist. This, because the second leg is a long leg and often against the wind. He carries the baton in his left hand and runs on the outside of his lane. He puts the baton into the right hand of the third runner in the second take-over zone. Because he started running from the start of his own acceleration zone, and "ideally" will pass the baton 5m before the end of the second take-over zone, he will have sprinted 20m + 100m + 5m (125)m), even if he has only *carried* the baton approximately 100m. (Figure 18)

3. The third athlete must have similar qualities to those of the second leg athlete but must, in addition, be a good bend runner. He carries the baton in his right hand and keeps to the inside of his lane. He puts the baton into the left hand of the fourth ("anchor") runner in the third take-over zone. The distance he will run (125m) and carry the baton (100m) are as for the second runner. (figure 18)

4. The fourth athlete must be a confident, controlled "fighter" under pressure. He carries the baton in his left hand and holds the outside of his lane. Although he runs 120m in total, only 95m are run with the baton in his hand. (figure 18)

Sprint relays coaching stresses speed of baton through the box as the priority concept. Only then is there concern over the method of passing the baton. Athletes work on reacting to visual cues; on running flat out through the box (incoming athlete); or out of the box (outgoing athlete).

Coaching Points

The idea of reacting to a visual cue might be developed with the beginner running when a rolling ball reaches a mark on the track. The sprint relay athlete must react to an incoming athlete reaching a predetermined mark on the track — a "check mark". The precise position of the check mark for a given two athletes is specific to these athletes. The following may help coaches and athletes establish sound check marks.

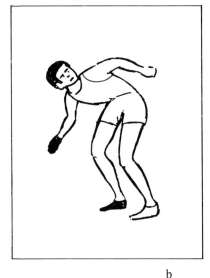

a
b

Figure 19

(1) *The Beginner Athlete:*

    a.   He should not use the acceleration zone.

    b.   He should use an upright start (figure 19a) or semi crouch (19b).

    c.   He should start with 16 pigeon (heel-toe) steps as check mark; then

          — if the incoming athlete runs past him — open it to 20, or

          — if the incoming athlete doesn't reach him — reduce it to 12.

    e.   He will not be able to perform many "trials" — and the "errors" will be many! Several training units may be required.

    f.   There will also be lack of consistency in speed of approach and of starting.

    g.   Switch "partners" only in an emergency in practice and competition.

    h.   The keynote will be, for this level of relay team, safety rather than "the risk business"!

    i.   The coach should note all check marks.

(2) *The Developing Athlete*

    a.   He should use the start of the acceleration zone as the check mark, and use 20 pigeon steps into the zone to locate *his* starting position.

    b.   He should eventually use the full 10m of the acceleration zone and place the check mark 25 pigeon steps before (figure 20).

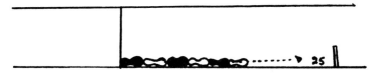

Figure 20

Check marks are normally measured in "pigeon steps" (i.e. heel to toe) and reasonable mark to start with is 25.

Figure 21

Figure 22

c. He will gradually be introduced to the modified crouch start (figure 21) with a preference established for this form of start — or the semi crouch (figure 19b). The latter is becoming more popular at International level.

d. The check mark should be *very* visible — white adhesive tape 5-10cm wide and 30cm long; or two strips 20cm apart, each 5cm wide and 30cm in length, are fairly widely used. (figure 22). Safety pins should be used to hold down the tape in wet weather.

e. Adjustments to check marks are again by trial and error — opening or reducing it in the light of experience.

f. There will be increasing consistency and training units should be kept brief and frequent. This should help reinforce the learning process whilst reducing the interference of fatigue.

g. Whilst "sound and safe" will be the main criteria in coaching, the athletes must now be encouraged to have confidence in their colleagues and to sprint as if in individual events.

h. When occasion permits, athletes should be moved around in practice sessions, to establish options for replacements in the event of injury.

i. The coach should note all check marks.

(3)   The Advanced Athlete

a. Check marks will move out to around 30 pigeon steps.

b. Competition is the critical focus of training, with most relevant adjustments made on evaluation of competition performance.

c. There will be clear understanding on the type of change to be used, and on the individual athlete's preference for semi or modified crouch start.

d. There is a move towards the fine dividing line between safety and risk.

e. All check marks should be noted by the coach, with relevant adjustments for prevailing conditions also listed.

f. Alternative line-ups and reserves must be planned for and coached.

Methods of Baton Change

In 4 × 100m, the baton change is "non-visual". Once the outgoing/receiving athlete has seen the incoming/giving athlete hit the check mark, he starts as if reacting to the gun in an individual sprint race. The incoming athlete calls *"HAND"* when he can pass the baton. The outgoing athlete puts back his hand; the incoming athlete puts the baton into his hand — and the change is complete. The outgoing runner does *not* watch the baton into his hand — hence "non-visual". In 4 × 100m it is the incoming athlete's responsibility to *give* the baton.

Two different types of baton change, have emerged at international level:—

(1)   Downsweep (Figure 23) (eg. U.S.A., G.B.)

This type affords considerably greater free distance than the others. There are difficulties for the outgoing athlete in keeping the hand steady. Practice should, however, make the change possible in 1-2 strides. The incoming athlete must place the baton downwards and firmly into the outgoing athlete's palm. No adjustment of baton is necessary for the next change.

Figure 23
(downsweep)

Figure 24
(upsweep)

Figure 25

(2)   Upsweep (Figure 24) (e.g. G.D.R., U.S.S.R.)

This is certainly the safest type of change and can be executed most "naturally" within the sprinting action. Practice quickly makes it possible to make the change in 1-4 strides. The incoming athlete must place the baton firmly upwards into the "V" between the thumb and hand. Adjustment of the baton is frequently necessary.

A modification of downsweep is a "push forward" into a hand angled downwards from the normal downward receiving position. (Figure 25).

At international level there has been a substantial shift between 1980 and 1990 from upsweep to the downsweep and push forward. Whatever type is used — the key focus of the coach's work is to ensure that—

— The baton loses no speed through the box.

— The passes are confident and safe.

— The athletes continue to work on sprint performance development.

The measure of technical efficiency of the relay team is the differential between the time recorded by the team and the sum of their individual 100m times in that season. A good rule of thumb will be a target of 1.5 - 2.0 secs for clubs and 2.5 - 3.0 secs for international teams.

Coaching Points

(1)   The coach selects a type of change — say downsweep.

(2)   Athletes work in groups of four — numbered 1, 2, 3, 4.

(3)   Athletes standing and walking, put back correct hand on the call "HAND"

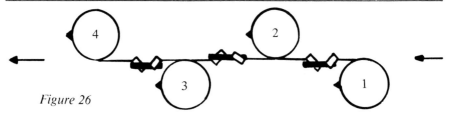

Figure 26

a .   All athletes walk, jog or run at the same pace

b .   Athlete 1 calls "hand" and passes baton to athlete 2. (right to left hand)

c .   Athlete 2 calls "hand" and passes baton to athlete 3. (Left to right hand)

d .   Athlete 3 calls "hand" and passes baton to athlete 4 (right to left hand)

e .   Athlete 4 drops baton onto the track, all athletes continue to move forward and athlete 1 picks up baton ready to repeat a-b-c-d.

(4) Athletes walk in line (number 4 at front, followed by 3, 2, 1). Athlete 1 carries baton in right hand — calls hand; athlete 2 puts back hand; athlete 1 places baton down into the presented hand. This is repeated through to athlete 4. He drops baton on ground; the column keeps walking; and athlete 1 picks up baton. The drill is repeated (figure 26).

(5) Drill (4) is performed at a jog then at a run.

(6) This drill can be sophisticated further by two athletes working at a sprint. The baton is not, however, dropped but is passed backwards.

(7) Check marks are located, on the track at the first take-over zone. 1st and 3rd changes can be rehearsed together. 2nd change is done separately.

(8) Athletes work on changes at a jog, then at ½-¾ speed, then full speed.

(9) The next stage is competition itself.

6.20 4 × 400m

The concept of working to ensure no loss of baton speed through the box still holds good in the longer relay, even if at a less sophisticated level. The method of change is visual. The outgoing athlete judges when to commence his run against the speed of the incoming athlete. He then takes the baton from the incoming runner whilst on the move and, clearly, with his eye on the baton. The outgoing athlete faces inward and reaches his left hand back towards the incoming athlete, palm towards the inside of the track. (Figure 27). The incoming athlete has the baton in his right hand and "presents" it for the outgoing runner to take on the move.

The outgoing runner then "kicks" out of the box into his race pace — changing the baton from the left hand to the right. In the 4 × 400m it is the outgoing athlete's responsibility to *take* the baton.

Figure 27

(1) The first runner remains in lane for 400m — but the stagger is for 500m. In other words, it is approximately the 400m stagger plus the 200m stagger. This gives the athlete a clear run — but the greater stagger can be disconcerting. He runs a flat-out leg. (note:— Where there are only three or two teams, the athlete may only be required to run the first bend in lanes — as for the 800m start).

49

Figure 28   a   b

Figure 29

(2)   The second athlete takes the baton in lane and remains for one bend in lane. He must learn not to settle for a following role after the "break" line. He must be fully committed to running through 200m — consistent with a full out 400m run — applying himself especially to the 100m - 300m section of the leg. He runs a flat out leg. (note:— Where the first athlete has only run the first bend in lane, the change is as for the 2nd athlete to 3rd athlete.) The athletes running legs 2 and 3 should endeavour to get into 1st, 2nd or 3rd place by the time they get to the 200m mark. This is because, by I.A.A.F. rules, the *next* athlete in their team may position himself in the "box" from lane 1 outwards according to the team's race position at the 200m mark. So a team placed, say, second at 200m may assume the second position outside the athlete whose team leads at 200m. No "receiving" athlete may change his position once the "200m" order is decided.

(3)   The third athlete stands in a jostling line (figure 28) — moving as close to the inside of the track as possible — or rather as opposing athletes will allow! He must endeavour to "make room" for the incoming second athlete by holding off the athlete inside him with his right hand; and the athlete outside him by sticking out his seat! (Figure 29) He takes the baton and kicks out of the box, whilst also taking care to avoid other fast moving or staggering opponents. He runs a flat out leg.

(4)   The final change is as for the second. This athlete races to capitalise on the contribution of the first three athletes; his own strengths; and on the weaknesses of his opposion. He may have to think through this leg tactically — so must have the capacity to do so. Normally he

50

will be the fastest of the quartet, and probably the most experienced but this will depend on the overall team strategy. More accurately, then, the anchor leg athlete is selected as the best athlete for that leg, bearing in mind the overall team strengths, and those of the opposition.

(5) Running Order:—

First — Must be fast enough to ensure no loss of contact. The team must not be out of the race after the first leg!

— Thought might then be given to putting in the athlete with least experience of 4 × 400m because there are not the distractions of physical contact, broken pace and so on. However, he will not necessarily be the slowest in the team.

Second — Strong and committed athlete with confidence to run his own race.

Third — A fair bit of experience is required on this leg to reduce to a minimum the problems for the last leg runner. This is the team's last chance to get into the race. It must not be left to the anchor athlete to pull back the opposition *and* race for the honours. If he has to do the former, there will be no energy for the latter!

Athletes at club level should learn the problems of each leg. Too often the 4 × 400m squad which arrives at international level is a group of last leg runners!

Fourth — The last leg is for the best last leg athlete. This may sound obvious, but there will occasionally be a situation where, on paper, the last leg athlete is not the fastest of the quartet. Coaches are sometimes tempted at this point to stick to the rule "fastest runs last". This can be a serious error of judgement. The decision must come down to what is best for the team to produce a result. The decision may not always be popular and can lead to occasional disappointed athletes — but the coach *must* take the lead in such matters; must carefully balance the qualities of each athlete and contribution to the team performance; must evaluate the strengths and weaknesses of the opposition; and must go for the team most likely to produce the best result.

It is difficult to afford a guide to the technical efficiency of a given 4 × 400m relay team. If the team is clear of opposition after the first two legs, the second and third changes afford clear runs through the box and little or no potential loss of baton speed through bumping and boring etc. The differential in this instance should, therefore, be greater than when the athletes are involved in jostling at the take-over. On the other hand, when the race is close over each leg, the athletes may be drawn to faster times. However, the 1984 GDR women's World Record of 3.15.92, with clear runs through the box produced a differential of 1.09 sec; whilst the 1984

U.K Men's European and Commonwealth record of 2.59.13, with considerable physical contact, produced a differential of 4.36 secs! Normally, the 2nd, 3rd and 4th athletes with a rolling start and given a reasonably clear run are worth 0.5-1.0 secs per leg, giving a team differential of 1.5-3 secs.

Coaching Points

(1)   The best introduction, for athletes up to 15 or 16 years old, to the 4 × 400m event is to run relays such as 4 × 200m or 4 × 300m. This will familiarise them with the problems of jostling, visual changes and so on; and will at the same time capture the excitement of this event.

(2)   The outgoing athlete works to judge the pace of the incoming athlete to take the baton without loss of speed. This is done first at a walk and then at a jog.

(3)a. Athletes are divided into teams of five for continuous relays over 400m.

Runner 1 —	starts and runs to the first *4 × 100m* relay box.
Runner 2 —	takes the baton at the first *4 × 100m* relay box and runs to the second *4 × 100m* relay box.
Runner 3 —	takes the baton at the second *4 × 100m* relay box and runs to the third *4 × 100m* relay box.
Runner 4 —	takes the baton at the final *4 × 100m* relay box and runs to the *4 × 400m* relay box.
Runner 5 —	takes the baton at the *4 × 400m* relay box and runs to the first *4 × 100m* relay box, etc.

   b.   A steady fixed pace is used — e.g. 72 secs per lap.

   c.   Athletes take baton in the left hand facing into the track, and transfer the baton to the right hand to carry it through the leg.

(4)   When the teams are coached for 4 × 400m, the coach must ensure that:

   — the incoming athlete's pace is consistent with that of a fatigued 400m athlete!

   — Athletes 3 and 4 are familiar with bumping and jostling in the box — "making space" and giving the incoming athlete a clear view of the outgoing athlete's hand.

   — Athletes 2, 3 and 4 *take* the baton from the incoming athlete.

   — Athletes 1 and 2 rehearse *their* change free from physical contact.

   — Athlete 2 works on commitment *beyond* the 200m mark.

   — Athletes 2 and 3 run for leading positions through 200m.

7.00 THE PREPARATION PROGRAMME

Preparation for 100m, 200m or 400m is a year-round programme — elaborated upon and developed over several years. As an athlete emerges from a pre-and early teen age phase of an all round fitness programme and experience of several events, he may move towards sprints as his speciality. Mid to late teens will see a gradual shift of 3-4 training days to 6 training days per week; and from 1-2 units of training per day towards 1-3 units of training per day. The athlete's progression through his "developmental" years might be as in Table 24.

7.10 General Points

The content of a sprinter's programme was suggested by Bill Marlow as the six "S" 's.

Strength —	This can be divided into *General* and *Specific*
Stamina — (Endurance)	This can be divided into *General* and *Specific*. These two areas of preparation on the one hand develop the athlete's general capacity to accept specific training loads; and on the other, develop the athlete's specific fitness for his event.
Skill — (Technique)	The athlete seeks to express himself through his technique. Sound technique is therefore essential, but can only be built on that foundation of basic (general) fitness which will enable the athlete to perform a sound technique without compensatory movements.
Speed —	Once basic fitness and sound technique are established, the athlete progresses specific fitness which will make technique more effective and learns to express that technique at speed. Speed of execution must not, however, compromise the technique. Speed is, then, a sophistication of technique.
Suppleness — (Mobility)	This is general for therapeutic and regenerative parts of the annual training programme, but its regular "maintenance" is specific to the sprinter's needs.
(P) *Sychology!* —	This embraces relating the athlete's multi-faceted personality to the demands of competitive sprinting. It operates at the extremes of loading — (1) Competitive ability (2) Relaxation, Regeneration, Recovery.

The detail of such content may take any of several forms, but the following is suggested as the shape of training units which are known to have been effective. Coaches and athletes may wish to try these, then adapt, add to or eliminate in the light of experience.

TABLE 24

AN ATHLETE'S DEVELOPMENTAL PROGRESSION

Year	Age	Training days/week	Training units/week	Objective	Type of Training Emphasis	Status
1-4	12-15	3	3-5	General athletic base	General athletic activity	—
5	16	4	4-6	Sound athletic base	General conditioning	Regional Age Group
6	17	4-5	4-8	Sound athletic base	General conditioning — commence specialisation	,,
7	18	5	5-8	Specific athletic base	Year plan-specialist	National Age Group
8	19	5-6	5-10	Specific athletic progression	,,	,,
9	20	6	6-12	,,	,,	National Senior
10	21	6	6-12	,,	,,	,,
11	22	6	6-12	Stability of specific athletic base	Year plan-general and specialist	,,
12	23	6	6-12	Specific athletic progression *(breakthrough)*	Year plan-specialist	Inter-National Ranking
13	24	6	6-12	Regeneration and stability of specific fitness	Year plan-general and specialist	,,
14	25	6	6-12	Specific athletic progression	Year plan specialist	,,

etc.

7.20   STRENGTH — GENERAL

1.   The purpose of general strength work is to evaluate the athlete's all round balanced basis of strength. On the one hand this equips him to learn his basic sprint techniques; on the other, it is a platform for development of specific strength.

7.21 CIRCUIT TRAINING — Figure 30

C Circuit

Dosage	Exercise	Repetitions	
If included normally done 2-6 times per week over 2-4 weeks introduction block. Sometimes done instead of stage in basic block.	Press-ups	50% max.	Progression:— is by number of circuits per session. Increased by 1 every week, commencing with 3 circuits. Two minutes recovery between circuits. Maximum number of circuits 6. Retest for maximum if continued beyond 4 weeks. Also consider competing against the clock after 4 weeks
	Burpees	50% max. in 45 secs.	
	Curls (abd.)	50% max. in 60 secs.	
	Broken Cradles	50% max. in 60 secs.	
	Pull-ups	50% max.	
	Speedball	8 × 60 secs.	

Recovery: 2 mins between circuits. No rest between exercises.

7.22 WEIGHT TRAINING — Figure 31

A Weights (B.W. = Body weight)

Dosage	Exercise/Repetitions	
If included — normally done 2 times per week, over 6-8 weeks in basic block.	Cleans. $3 \times 8 \times 75\%$ B.W. Bench Pr. $3 \times 8 \times 75\%$ B.W. ½ Squat $3 \times 8 \times 100\%$ B.W. Bent Knee) $3 \times 10 \times 20\%$ B.W. Sit-up) $3 \times 10 \times 20\%$ B.W. Hip lift $3 \times 10 \times 40\%$ B.W.	Progression:— mainly speed of operation. N.B. Suggest % B.W. represents reasonable target for athletes after initial work learning techniques. For developing or advanced athletes, loads should be 65%-75% maximum.

Recovery: 2-4 mins between sets and exercises.

7.23 STAGE TRAINING — Figure 32

S Stage

Dosage	Exercise	Repetitions	
Normally done 3-6 times per week over 6-8 weeks in basic block.	Press-ups	8×15)	Progression:— (a) by reps. and sets
	½ Squat	8×25)	(b) by using weights jacket
	Chinnies	8×25)	(c) by "jumping"
	Hip rotate	$4 \times 2 \times 8$)	progressed per week. *e.g.*
	Treadmill	4×25)	*Wk.* 1 2 3 4 5 6 7 8
	Speedball	8×2mins	Progression: a a b c a a b c

Progression in time and sets per week.

Recovery: 30 secs between sets and exercises.

Figure 30

Organisation of circuit and stage training. (See also Fig. 32)

TESTING

maximum
= A repetitions

maximum in
45 secs.
= B repetitions

maximum in
60 secs.
= C repetitions

maximum
= D repetitions

maximum in
45 secs.
= E repetitions

maximum in 60 secs.
= F repetitions

$\dfrac{A}{2 \text{ reps}}$

$\dfrac{B}{2 \text{ reps}}$

CIRCUIT TRAINING

$\dfrac{F}{2 \text{ reps}}$

$\dfrac{C}{2 \text{ reps}}.$

$\dfrac{E}{2 \text{ reps}}$

$\dfrac{D}{2 \text{ reps}}$

Circuit Training

For each exercise in the circuit, the athlete performs a set of repetitions, then moves on immediately to the next exercise.

If more than one circuit is to be attempted, then there should be 2 mins. recovery between circuits.

Normal number = 3-5 circuits.

Figure 31

Weight training requires supervision to ensure sound technique in pursuit of safety and efficiency.

Weight training is based on orthodox weight training techniques and equipment.

Figure 32

Stage training

At each exercise, the athlete performs all sets of repetitions, with 30 secs.
recovery between sets, then moves on to the next exercise "stage". 30 secs.
recovery is taken between stages, until all are completed.

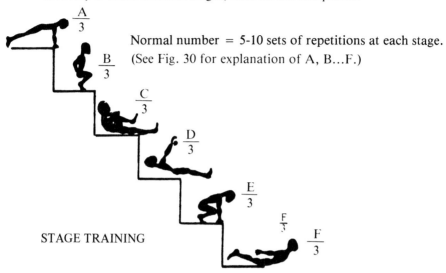

Normal number = 5-10 sets of repetitions at each stage.

(See Fig. 30 for explanation of A, B...F.)

STAGE TRAINING

7.30 STRENGTH — SPECIFIC

The purpose of specific strength work is to develop the types of strength
most consistent with the strength demands of sprinting. For example, the
100m sprinter requires strength for drive and the elasticity of stride and
lift; while the 400m sprinter also requires strength for maintaining elasticity in stride and lift in a world of accumulating endurance factors.

100m, 200m, 400m. — a specific strength training unit comprises exercises such as
these:—

Heavy harness runs (20-25kg.) (Figure 33)	4 × 25m-30m	Progression by increasing number of repetitions through to 6 maximum.
"Skip B" — (High Knees) (Figure 34)	4 × 25m	Progression by increasing distance through to 100m or more.
Power Run — (Speed bound) (Figure 35)	4 × 25m	Progression by increasing distance through to 100m maximum.
Light harness runs (10-15kg.) (Figure 36)	4 × 30m from rolling 30m.	Progression by increasing number of repetitions through to 8 maximum.

"Skip A" — (High Knees) (Figure 37)	4 × 20m	Progression by increasing number of repetitions through to 8 maximum.
10 Bounds + 20-30m run out (Figure 38)	4 repetitions	May remain as a fixed control or progress by increasing the number of repetitions to 6 max.
Rebounds over hurdles (Figure 39)	4 × 6	Progression by i. increasing the number of repetitions to 6 maximum. ii. increasing the number of hurdles. iii. increasing the height of hurdles.
Highland fling (Figure 40) (alternate split rebounds)	3 × (4 × 6)	Progression by increasing the number of repetitions to 4 × 10 max; and the number of sets to 5 max.
40m steep hill or steps	4 repetitions	Progression by increasing the number of repetitions to 6 maximum.
Strides	4 × 100m	Progression by increasing the number of repetitions to 6 maximum.

Figure 33

Figure 34   a   b   c   d

58

Figure 35

Figure 36

Figure 37

Figure 38

Figure 39

a

b

c

d

Figure 40

59

Figure 41

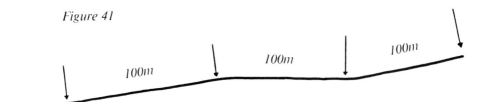

400m Only — The 400m athlete may include some of the above and one of the following in a given specific strength training unit.

100m — 500m shallow hills	4 repetitions	Progression by increasing i. the length of hill ii. The number of repetitions to 6 maximum.

* Alternatively, the specific strength programme for a 400m athlete may have one unit per week from the above group of exercises; and a second weekly unit may be one of the following:—

100m - 300m varied gradient hills (e.g. — medium gradient-flat-shallow gradient) (Figure 41)	4 repetitions	Progression by increasing the number of repetitions.
200m-400m light harness runs	4 repetitions	Progression by increasing i. the distances ii. the number of repetitions.

Note:— The coach must carefully select the athlete's specific strength training unit to a limit of 6-8 exercises, varying the muscle actions and dynamics involved. This work is *very* demanding and can place extremes of loading on the athlete. It must only be included in an athlete's programme when the athlete has a well developed general strength and endurance base.

7.40 ENDURANCE — GENERAL (aerobic)

The purpose of general endurance work is to raise the athlete's aerobic capacity.

A general endurance training unit may be any one of the following:—

Fartlek

Diagonals	e.g.	16 × diagonal of soccer pitch; jog goal line recovery.
Timed runs — steady pace	e.g.	3 × 4 × 60 sec. run — walk 60 sec recovery between repetitions; 5 mins between sets.
Game	e.g.	Basketball; Squash.

Circuit and Stage must also be considered as contributing to general endurance.

"Sweat sessions" — general activity unit for 45-60 minutes.

7.41   ENDURANCE — SPECIFIC

The purpose of specific endurance work is to develop the types of endurance most consistent with the endurance demands of sprinting. The 100m athlete is essentially reliant on his alactic anaerobic energy source, as is the 200m athlete. However, the latter must also look to lactic anaerobic energy provision, even if not to the same considerable extent as the 400m athlete who also seeks access to a substantial aerobic reservoir. In practice, sprinters should include work for development of all three energy pathways. Each athlete will, however, require to lean towards the bias of demand for his event.

A specific endurance training unit may be any of the following:

100m. 200m. 400m.
At sub. maximal pace

Progression by increasing pace of run weekly	At maximal or near maximal pace	
7 × 200m (Recovery 3m.2m.1m.3m.2m.1m.)	Time trial 200m	
2 × 3 × 300m (recovery 3 min//10 min)	2-3 × 300m	full recovery (or for 400m -2-3 × 300m fixed recov.)
2-3 × 3 × 250m (recovery 2½ min//10m)	2-3 × 250	,, ,,
3 × 3 × 150m (recovery 2m/10m)	2-3 × 150m	,, ,,
*3 × (150m-120m-90m) (Recovery 2//10m)	150;120;90	time trials
*3 × (120-90-60) (Recovery 2//10m)	120:90:60	,, ,,
* 100-150-200-250-200-150-100 (Recovery 2m,3m,4m,5m,4m,3m,)	250:150:100	,, ,,

*Paces established on basis of slower pace for longer distance.

Pace varying sub-maximal — maximal according to focus of unit

3 × 3 × 150 (30m ¾ speed drive: 30m easy stride; 30m ¾ speed lift: 30m easy stride: 30m ¾ speed lift)

6 × 200m (80m easy drive: 30m fast lift: 90m hold pace and stride)

3 × 4 × 120m (30m drive: 30m stride: 30m lift: 30m stride).

400m

At sub-maximal pace	At maximal or near maximal pace
2 × 300m: 3 × 200m: 4 × 150m: 6 × 100m (Recovery 3min:5min:2min:5min: 1½min:5min:1min)	Long. Clock:— 100m-200m-300m-200m-100m full recovery.
3-5 × 500m or 600m (Recovery 5min or 6min)	Time Trial 500m or 600m
4-6 × 400m differential — controlled pace to 200m; 2-4 secs faster for second 200m. (Recovery 5-10min)	*Control run:*— eg. 30 secs 1st 200: flat out 2nd 200:
3-6 × mid-section 400m — controlled pace to 100m; target time *next* 200m; stride last 100m. (Recovery time 5-10m)	*Control run:* eg. target competition pace for mid 200.
"20 second runs" — athlete runs 20 secs flat out — distance recorded.	
This distance less 10-15 metres is now marked as the training distance	20 sec. run. Time trial.

athlete tries to achieve
the training distance at 90 sec intervals
as often as possible.
Unit stops when athlete is down by 10m.

		At maximal	
		2-3 × 300m	fixed recovery.
		or	
Turnabouts	3-4 × (4 × 80m) (Recovery 5mins)	2-3 × 250 or	'' ''
Back to Backs	3-4x (4 × 100m) (Recovery 30 sec/5mins)	2-3 × 200 or	'' ''
Screwdriver	3-4 × (100m(30sec) 80m (20sec) 60m (10secs)40m (Recovery:— 5min)	1 × 300m)) +)	'' ''
Mixed Grill *e.g.*	2-3 × (a 1 × 100-80-60-40 screwdriver) (rest 60 secs) (b Rolling 150m-200m.	1 × 200m) etc.	'' ''

7.50 TECHNIQUE

Although the coach will put to the athlete relevant current technical models, he must eventually work to sophisticate the athlete's own interpretation of these models. The technique models become, as it were, the "ground rules" with which the athlete's interpretation must comply. This is clearly seen in the variety of sprint starts and running actions witnessed at, say, an Olympic Final. These athletes are the best in the world, separated only by hundredths of a second, yet they have their own versions of sprinting. Consequently, it is difficult to deduce that one athlete's technique is "wrong" and another's "right". The coach must clearly understand the key features of the technical models in sprinting and, keeping within the "ground rules", seek to maximise the athlete's potential through the athlete's interpretation. This is the broad purpose of technique training.

Sub-Maximal Pace

Note: The coach should encourage the athlete to make conscious effort in *all* track work to maintain sound technique.

Technique work requires that

— the athlete is not fatigued before or during the unit of training.
— the squad should not enter into a competition situation.
— the coach concentrates on clear technique training objectives; — it is preferable that he should have occasional access to video equipment.
— the facilities are conducive to sound technique (i.e. synthetic running surface; dry; warm; etc.)

A technique training unit may be any one of the following:

3 × 4 × 30m Block work at ½ speed — ¾ speed working on distance covered in 10 strides.

3 × 4 × 60m Build ups to ¾ speed.

3 × 4 × 40m Rolling ¾ speed.

3 × 3 × 60m-120m Speed change at ½-¾ — full.

2-3 × 3-4 × 120m Bend work — easy build up 60m + 30m lift: 30m stride.

Technique Drills:—   3-5 Skip B × 20-30m
                                   3-5 Skip A × 10m
                                   3-5 ½ speed pike position as in driving (figure 42)
                                   3-5 × 10 stride straight leg runs (figure 43)
                                   3-5 × 20 stride hip swinging. (figure 44)

4 × 100m Relay training units at ½-¾ pace.

Figure 42

Figure 43

Figure 44

a   b

7.60   SPEED

Maximal and near maximal pace extension of technique is the basis of speed work.

It is preferable that, in speed training units, the running surface is synthetic. Weather should be dry and warm — or, alternatively, indoors should be used. Speed work should take advantage of the prevailing conditions e.g. following wind etc.

—   Squad handicap blockwork. e.g. 3-5 × 30m *or* 2-3 × 60m.
—   3 × 4 × 60m ¾ — full speed.
—   3 × 4 × 30m rolling — full speed run at the line.
—   Towing, elastic rope pull, downhill runs, strong following wind support.. in units of 2-3 × 3-6 × "activity". (Figure 45)
—   4 × 100m Relay competitions.
     Speed drills:— 6-10 repetitions "Ratatats" (Figure 46)
                         6-10 repetitions "Tripling" (Heel flicks at speed to kick seat.)
                         6-10 repetitions rapid pace to 40m roll-out.
                         Reaction games to sound and visual cues.

Figure 45

a. Towing

Athlete is obliged to move legs faster by being towed behind a motor-cycle at a speed 0,1-0,3 secs faster than the athlete's best for a rolling 30m. The pace is held for 20m-30m following a gradual build up to max speed over 60m-70m.

b. Elastic Pull

This method, first used in U.S.S.R in the late '60's to early '70's, has been replaced by an alternative method which is believed to be safer but lacks an inbuilt control. Two assistants/coaches pull tubular elastic to full stretch and the athlete is virtually "catapulted" over the first 10m. from a standing or crouch start.

c. Downhill Sprinting

Downhill sprinting on a hill of 15° maximum decline is probably the most widely used of forced leg speed training units. 30m maximum distance should be used following 40m-60m build up of speed.

NOTE:

1. Methods a, and b, can be dangerous and *must not* be used with athletes under 18 years.

2. For the same reason — such training *must be supervised by an experienced BAAB senior coach.*

3. The safest method is c, — but again it requires supervision and is best for athletes over 18 years.

4. Leg speed work for younger athletes is best limited to leg-speed drills such as "triplings", "ratatats" etc.

5. Deceleration on completing the training distance must be gradual.

a   b

Figure 46

7.70 MOBILITY

Mobility is dealt with in detail in the B.A.A.B. Mobility Training booklet. However, it is worth stressing here that the sprinter *must* maintain throughout the year a good range of movement in the hip and shoulder region and should work the trunk through its movement potential at least once per week. Hamstrings, calves, adductors and the full range of arm action must receive daily attention.

7.80 PSYCHOLOGY

Competitive Ability training units are clearly linked to the speed training units. In fact, one of the key values of squad training is that there is inbuilt competition in all training units where the athletes work together. The nature of competition ranges from the inter-personal banter to the occasional "needle" in track units! Whatever, the coach should be aware of, rather than force, the learning process that such situations represent. The sharpest focus of competition attitude training is, of course, competition itself and consequently time trials, handicap races and introductory/low level competitions bring the athlete to the sharper end of this aspect of training. Coaches must take careful note of the athlete's performance in such situations. This means rather more than noting the times! It suggests comment on how the athlete handled the pre-competition period; how he handled different race situations; how he reacted to his time/result — and so on.

Regeneration, Relaxation and Recovery training units are essential inclusions in the training programme. The coach must build into the programme:—
— recovery times (in minutes/seconds) etc., within a training unit.
— recovery periods (in days) between the athlete experiencing the *same* type of training.

- relaxation periods (in days) between and after units of high intensity before a competition.
- regeneration periods (in days) after a major competition.
- regeneration periods (in weeks) after a major season.
- etc.

The coach should also be aware of those activities, environments etc., which will afford regeneration, relaxation and recovery. They actually vary from athlete to athlete, and might include:
- sunshine and swimming   or   cool woodlands, hills and walking.
- upbeat music   or   soft, reflective music.
- vigorous deep massage   or   gentle superficial massage.
- a hot sauna   or   a warm salt bath
- "aerobics"/exercise to music   or   autogenic training
- a social game with a frisbee   or   an easy "private" jog.
- etc.

This whole "psychology" area is less "tangible" than the other training areas. The coach, athlete, physiotherapist, sports psychologist, parents, wife/husband, friends, other coaches and so on all share in the input which will help the coach make decisions in this part of the programme.

7.90   DRAWING IT TOGETHER

Although there are obviously many variations on a theme, in order to illustrate the general idea of planning the year for 100m 200m or 400m athletes, figure 47 is offered as a double periodised approach (indoor and outdoor season) or a single periodised approach (outdoor season only) to a season where the major competition is in the week commencing 25th August; and the selection conditions must be met between the week commencing 30th June and the end of the week commencing 21st July.

Bearing in mind the general guidelines to programme construction as set out in the B.A.A.B. book 'Training Theory', together with the various examples of training units etc., as listed above, the coach should pursue training objectives through his programme detail along the following lines. (Table 25).

FIGURE 47
YEAR PLAN

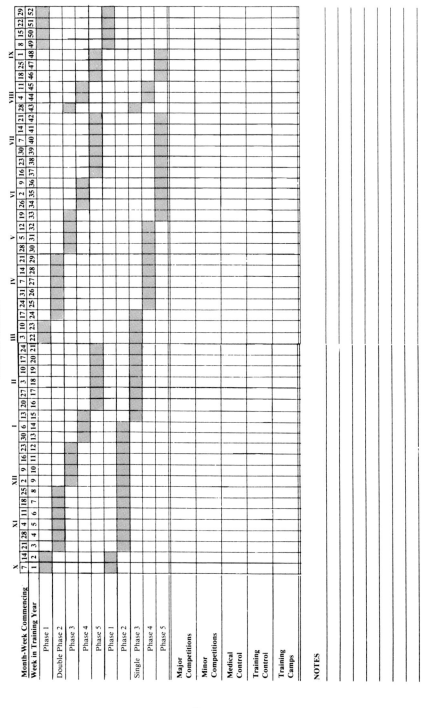

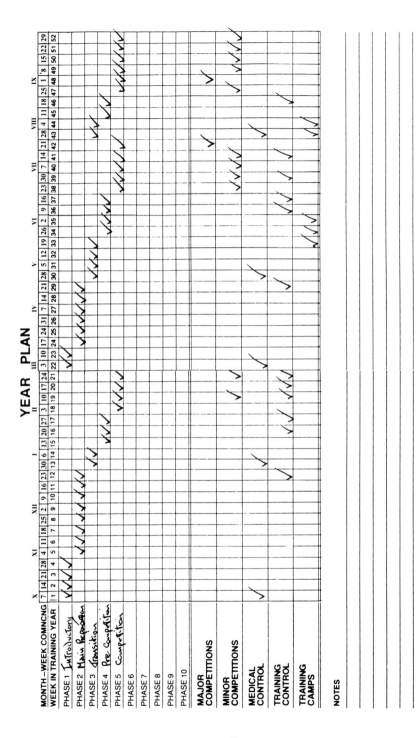

Figure 47 Detail a

Possible interpretation of a double periodized year using a short 4-week indoor season.

69

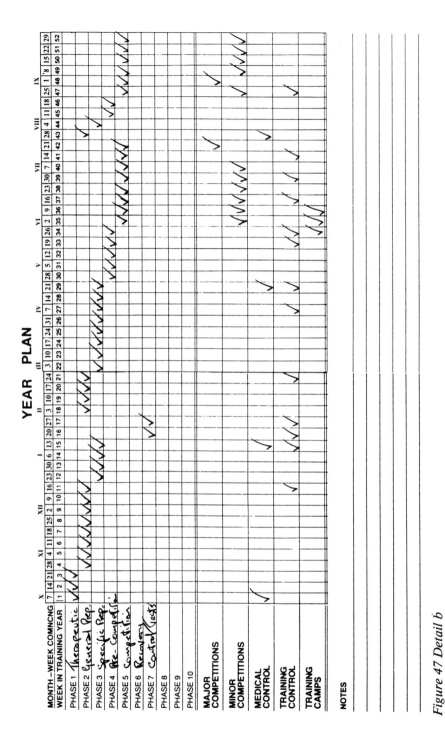

Figure 47 Detail b

Possible interpretation of a single periodized year using a two week control period mid-winter

TABLE 25

MAIN TRAINING OBJECTIVES

	Phase 1	Phase 2	Phase 3
100,200 400m.	General Endurance	Specific Endurance (sub.max)	Specific Endurance (sub.max) (max.)
	General Strength	General Strength (develop)	Specific Strength (maintain) (see 400)
	Mobility	Specific Strength (develop)	
	Regeneration/ Recovery		General Strength (maintain)
			Technique
	Establish Routine		Competitive Ability
			Regeneration/ Recovery.
400m only		General Endurance	Specific Strength (develop)
			General Endurance.

	Phase 4	Phase 5
100,200 400m.	SPEED	SPEED
	Competitive Ability (occasional)	Competitive Ability
	Specific Endurance (maintain) (see 400)	Regeneration/Recovery/ Technique
	Specific Strength ('')	Specific Endurance (occasional, maintain)
	Regeneration/Recovery/ Relaxation.	Specific Strength (occasional, maintain)
	Technique	Competition Performance.
400 only	Specific Endurance (maintain)	Specific and General Endurance (occasional (maintain)
	Specific Strength (maintain)	

8.00 SPECIFIC EVENTS COMMENTS

Warm up is a blend of ritual and highly functional routine, unique to an athlete. Whatever the detail, it should be of 45-60m duration, commenced approximately 75 minutes prior to the competition starting time. Before the athlete starts his warm-up, it should be checked that the meeting is running to time. If not, establish the estimated revised time of start for the event.

The competition warm-up, whilst unique in detail, should normally assume the following general shape.

a — Jog and/or easy stride.
b — Stretching/mobility.
c — ¾ speed stride and technique revision.
d — Full pace work
e — Relax.

The training warm-up will, in sections c and d, be specific to the demands of the training unit.

After competition or training, the athlete should warm down for approximately 15 minutes using strides, easy stretch and jogging.

8.10 100m

— The coach will identify the pattern of the run as:—

Beginner and Developing:—   Start/Drive — Stride
                                 30-40m   — 70-60m.

Advanced :—   Start/Drive — Stride and lift.
                                 30-40m   — (70-60m)

The lift technique may or may not be used in a given race, but the advanced athlete must have it in his armoury.

— Consistent and fast reaction to the gun is essential, with reaction and start work being of critical importance in the pre-competition phase.
— As with all technique work, there should not be man to man competition until the techniques have stabilised for a given athlete.
— In squad work, athletes should work in handicap from blocks over time trial and racing distances.
— Athletes should be as familiar with reacting to being challenged (or "being run at") by opposition, as they are with challenging or "running at" the opposition.
— Athletes should learn to race several lanes away from, and in the next lane to, the main opponent. In major competition, an athlete can "choke" by concentrating so much on fighting the main opponent in the next lane that he forgets to run his own race.
— Athletes should be drilled for discipline in starting. Trying to "take a flyer" upsets the athlete himself as much as it irritates the opposition. Moreover, the penalty of a warning light on the athlete's blocks creates a bad mental attitude for the subsequent start. Finally, starters have memories like elephants for athletes who try "fliers"!
— The athlete should move quickly into the set position. An athlete can

occasionally be caught "on the rise" by a starter — and, in effect be left in the blocks.

— It is the starter's job to ensure a fair start. Ideally, this will coincide with the athlete's point of optimal concentration — around 2.2 secs.

In practice, the starter is usually around 2.1-2.3 — but he *will* wait till there's no movement. If this takes too long, he will ask the athletes to stand up. The following were the set — gun times in the 1983 World Championships 100m (Men and Women).

Holding time in Seconds	Number of starts
2.0	2
2.1	4
2.2	4
2.3	3
2.4	2
2.5	3
2.6	3
2.7	3
2.8	1

— Athletes must, then, in training be given long and short holds in the set position.

— Athletes must learn to check their blocks thoroughly before the race. As a discipline, then, in training 'strange' blocks should be used.

— Athletes must run *through* the finish line, just as a rugby player aims to get *over* the goal line rather than *to* it! Dipping, or turning a shoulder and leaning from the hip, should be rehearsed occasionally in time trials and build up competition but, as a rule, the technique is an emergency 'last measure' which is no replacement for quality sprinting through the line. If used, it must be executed over the last 1-2 strides — not before. The "grid" at the modern finish can be confusing. As a concept the athlete must not consider the grid to be the finish. He should work to get *beyond* it.

— In tournament competition, the athlete must always start fast enough in successive rounds to ensure that no excessive work demands are required mid to late race. To have to battle with such demands is energy and confidence sapping, and introduces the potential for hamstring injury.

The trick is to do enough to reach the final without letting the opposition know *exactly* what the athlete is capable of.

— Tournament competitions invariably involve athletes in early morning, high quality sprinting. This must be practised.

— If in doubt about what is required to qualify in a tournament, the athlete should treat every round as if it were a final.

— It should be borne in mind that in major tournaments the semi-finals and finals can be 1-1½ hours apart. This situation should be rehearsed, as must that of the "minimum" times allowed between rounds in competitions under AAA's laws.

— Irrespective of age, sex or experience, the athlete *must* warm-up and warm-down thoroughly and systematically before and after the race; before and after each round of a tournament; and before and after training. More than that, the athlete must wear clothing which will allow him to achieve an elevated body temperature *without* impeding movement.

Tights, close fitting warm-up suits, wet suits etc., must all be carefully chosen to fit the athlete's needs. The athlete should not warm-up in his competition vest. It is best that this is put on after warm up.

— Finally, the coach should ensure the athlete has check-ups with a physiotherapist and dentist; rapid access to a physiotherapist in the event of injury; and sound advice on diet.

8.20   200m

— The coach will recognise the need to work on a pattern of runs which is consistent with sound distribution of effort and energy over the distance. Consequently, a broad pattern such as this emerges:—

Beginner and Developing:—	Start/Drive — Stride 20-30m — 180-170m
Advanced:—	Start/Drive — Stride — Lift — Stride 20-30m — 60-50m— 30m— 90m.

— This will be interpreted in times as follows:—

	1st 100 time	2nd 100
Women	101-101.5% best 100m time	95-97.5% best 100m time
Men	102-102.5% "	94-96.0% "

— A consistent and fast reaction to the gun is important in the pre-competition phase.

— Technique work is very much as for 100m but with greater importance being placed on change of pace or kicking at speed.

— Athletes should "play" with their sprint technique armoury on the bend, off the bend and down the straight. For example, gradual build up to full pace over 80m-100m; working ¾ pace stride for 60m-80m — lifting to raise pace to full over 30m — then holding full pace stride for 30m-40m; working at ¾ pace over 120m — reacting to pace increase by training partners — etc.

— Athletes must, as an extension of this, learn to handle various situations or types of race in time trials and build up competitions. For example, if passed by an athlete on an inside lane on the bend, the athlete must learn to use *all* of the balance of the race to pull back, rather than try to win it back in an energy sapping 30-40 metres. Or again, if a bend is run faster than usual, the athlete must learn to maintain form without tension over what will appear to be a longer

straight than usual!
— Athletes must be familiar wth running in *any* lane. Coaches, for their part, must be *positive* and *constructive* in their evaluation of a given lane draw!
— The 100m advice on starting discipline also applies here. It may be worth noting that the holding time in 200m does vary slightly from that of 100m in terms of the possible range. Although the starter has a more difficult task at 200m, his objective is however the same. The following were the set-gun times in the 1983 World Championships 200m (Men and Women):—

Holding time in Seconds.	Number of Starts
1.9	1
2.0	0
2.1	2
2.2	3
2.3	5
2.4	2
2.5	5
2.6	2
2.7	3
2.8	0
2.9	2
3.0	1
3.1	2

— Athletes must, then, be afforded a very full range of starts in training.
— In addition to checking blocks thoroughly before the race, the athlete must experience "strange" blocks in training; must learn to angle the blocks appropriately for a given curve; and *must* be able to hear the starter's commands. In an outside lane, depending on the starter's position, this can sometimes be difficult. If necessary, the athlete must request louder commands.
— In warm up on the track, the athlete should jog round the bend after setting blocks to ensure that there are no obstacles in his lane.
— It is also of some value to stride the bend and simulate a light relaxed lift through the box.
— All other aspects of warm-up and warm-down are as for 100m.
— Early morning sprinting is required in tournament competitions — often the day after the 100m has been concluded. This must be practised.
— In tournament competition, the semi-finals and final may be only 90 mins. apart. This situation must be rehearsed, as must that of "minimum" time allowed between rounds in competitions under

A.A.A. Laws

— Also in tournament competition, the bend and the run off the bend in preliminary rounds must be fast enough to avoid unnecessary energy expenditure in the straight. Again, the idea is to run well enough in the heats and semi-final to get there without demonstrating personal strengths and weaknesses. Performance in the preliminary rounds is, of course, a means of getting to the final, but it is also part of the preparation for the final — physically and emotionally — and will be interpreted by the opposition in establishing *their* final game plan — just as analysis of the opposition's performance is part of the basis of the athlete's game plan.

— If in doubt in a tournament competition, each round should be treated as a final, with any easing of pace kept for late in the race.

— As in 100m, the athlete must be coached to run through the finish line.

— Finally the 200m athlete, like the 100m athlete, must look to the physiotherapy and nutrition aspects of the support programme, and have teeth checked regularly.

8.30 400m

— The coach will appreciate that this event is highly specialised as a sprint and endurance event, and consequently there is need to work on a most controlled pattern of run consistent with a sound distribution of effort and energy over the distance.

Consequently, a broad pattern such as this emerges:—

Beginner and Developing:—

Start/Drive — stride according to target pace — controlled stride in fatigue

| 20m-30m | — | 300m-290m | — | 80m |

Advanced:—

Start/Drive-controlled pace — stride according to target pace — controlled stride in fatigue

| 60m-80m | — | 260m-240m | — | 80m |

Any pace adjustment is based on modifications of drive or lift.

— This will be interpreted in times as follows:—

1st 200m time	2nd 200m time	Middle 200m
Women		
Best 200m + 1.5-2.0 sec	1st 200m + 1-1.5 sec	Best 200m + 2.0 secs.
Men		
Best 200m + 1.0-1.5 sec	1st 200m + 1-1.5 sec	Best 200m + 1.5 sec

— Commitment and fast reaction to the gun, whilst important, is located lower in the scale of priorities for 400m than for 200m or 100m. Of *far* greater importance is the athlete's capacity to:—
  — judge pace
  — adjust pace
  — maintain rhythm
  — control an efficient and effective stride in fatigue.
— The athlete must always check blocks and should experience "strange" blocks in training.
— Like the 200m athlete, the 400m specialist must play with the three variants of sprint technique in training. He must work on reacting to challenge; on "kicking off the front"; on lifting and/or picking up rhythm into and off bends; on varying pace in runs — such as in differential 300m (e.g. 200m in 32 secs + 100m flat out); on timing and pacing challenges to other athletes and so on.
— Athlete must learn to handle various situations or types of race in time trials or build up competitions. In particular he must learn that he has 400m to express his abilities; that sudden accelerations are costly; that clawing back an opponent's early lead is done gradually; and so on.
— Athletes must be familiar with racing in any lane, and must be just as disciplined in starting as the short sprint distance athlete.
— Because the athlete must from time to time encounter windy conditions, the coach should ensure that the athlete learns how to handle running into the wind, when judging the energy cost of the run is of more relevance than intermediate times. Here the athlete is not only equipping himself to deal with a combination of striding and driving, but is learning the *feel* of a given effort. He must learn to "listen" to his body.
— Tournament competitions normally require athletes to produce quality sprinting early in the morning — and to produce such quality on successive days — sometimes twice in one day — and with 4 × 400 to follow! This sort of race programme must be practised. Warm-up and warm-down routines and drills must be well established.
— In tournaments the athlete must be aware of the time required to qualify for a subsequent round, and must run a pace through 250m-300m which will permit a controlled and relaxed home straight stride. If qualifying is going to be tough, the coach must advise on the basis of the athlete's "best shot". If things go wrong, going out on a personal best, or close to it, will help make the experience a little more worthwhile.
— Finally, physiotherapy, dental and nutritional advice are critical aspects of an athlete's support programme.

8.40   4 × 100m

— The running pattern for each leg is really an extension of 100m sprints. The starting/driving and striding techniques, whether in reaction to the gun or an incoming athlete hitting the checkmark, are virtually as for 100m. The lifting technique is used by incoming athletes working into and through the box.

— Consistent and fast reactions are essential, whether to the gun or checkmark. Athletes should be sufficiently disciplined to ignore distractions which may interfere with consistency.

— The method of starting for 2nd, 3rd and 4th leg athletes — whether modified crouch or semi-crouch — once established, should always be adhered to.

— Baton change practices should be worked on without competition until the techniques are stable. Then the drills can be worked on in "competition" with other "pairs".

— The method of change must be well established and rehearsed regularly. Warming up, for team training and for competition, offers the ideal opportunity for such rehearsal.

— Their individual sprint events should equip them well vis-à-vis the sprinting portion of the event.

— The team should be familiar with running in any lane.

— First leg athletes should be familiar with the problem of the opposition's outgoing athlete immediately inside "overhanging" his lane in the modified crouch start position. There is possibility of collision here. This can also happen at the third change.

— Some third leg athletes start at outside of the lane and gradually cross over in the acceleration zone and first half of the take over zone. This, whilst sound in theory, can be dangerous in practice, and is only advised given extensive rehearsal.

— The team should — know the various relay track markings.
       — be on the track early to measure out check marks.
       — know the correct lane.
       — collect their checkmark tape (and safety pins if necessary) from the coach during relay warm-up.
       — check the checkmark distances with the coach during warm-up.
       — be sure that the checkmark is clearly visible.
       — keep an eye open for the signal to strip-off for the race.
       — rehearse the start position and run through the box once or twice.

— The first athlete must thoroughly check the blocks. The anchor athlete must run through the finish line.

— In developing a team the coach must work on safety and consistency as a basis for working towards faster times — with the associated risks.

— In tournaments there is a similar situation. The team must get "safely" into the final. Generally speaking, checkmarks are gradually 'opened' in the course of the tournament. More important, however, is that each round is used to help make decisions for the final. In major tournaments a video of each round is an invaluable evaluation tool as a basis for affording coaching advice for subsequent rounds.

— Because relays are at the end of a meeting or tournament, there is a possibility that injury will take an athlete out of the team. Not only must the coach have made plans for such an eventuality, and rehearsed the relevant changes, but the reserves must warm-up as part of the team. The team should always warm-up together.

— The coach should keep a careful note of observations *every* time the team runs out.

— All points made reference the individual sprints events should be noted.

— The athletes and coach must think and work as a team. This means frequent quality practices with full commitment and concentration.

8.50   4 × 400m

— The running pattern for each leg is as for 400m. Without doubt, however, athletes come to their 4 × 400m relay leg with a different attitude compared with the individual event. The attitude manifests itself in a rather more uninhibited approach to the run. The rhythm, changes of pace and so on have much more of the quality expressed in the competitiveness of sessions with colleagues. Training sessions where the athlete "plays" with speed, then, represent a very useful foundation for 4 × 400m relays.

— The individual 400m training programme equips them for running quality legs.

— The team members should be familiar with running in any lane and from any position.

— In tournament situations the athletes should know what level of performance is required to qualify for subsequent rounds, and adjust pace accordingly. The object is to have the best team to go for a result in the final. The rules allow 2 changes on the way through the tournament and although it can cause disappointment, these 2 changes should be used to ensure that all four athletes in the final team are at their best for the final. The team comes first. The preliminary rounds therefore become not only a means of getting into the final but they are also a means of helping get the best 4 in the final. The coach can check form, try a new running order, blood reserves and rookies in the atmosphere of the championships stadium, and so on. The coach can talk intentions and options but in the end, in making his decision, will disappoint those who are left out. The reserves and those who took the team to the final are all part of what makes the team great. They are all, then, "the team".

— The 4 × 400m squad, i.e. team plus reserves, should warm-up together and the coach must plan for replacements in the event of injury or illness. Whatever, no competition should arrive with unrehearsed changes.

— The coach should make a note of 4 × 400m splits every time the team runs. Apart from anything else, athletes like to have these.

- If the baton goes down, athletes must react fast to retrieve it and continue the run. There's at least one whole 'leg' to recover lost metres!
- All relevant points reference the individual event should be noted and applied.
- Finally, physiotherapy, dental and nutritional advice are essential aspects of the support programme.

8.60 60m INDOORS

- There is more pressure in this sprint than on any other! The start is all important but this is a "working" sprint from start to finish line. If the opposition gets away by 30m, it is unlikely that the athlete will come back unless he has immense control. The problem is that, with only 30m (less than 3 sec) to go, the athlete tightens. 30m and 60m from blocks and 30m rolling work are critical inclusions in the indoor pre-competition and competition period.
- Athletes should experience pressure in training, in races from 20m — 60m and in handicaps.
- This said, the athlete must be technically stable before being exposed to this very intense competition pressure.
- In tournament competitions the athlete must concentrate on quality starting in every round, and certainly must concentrate on his *own* race.
- Other advice is as for 100m.
- The 60m indoor session is a very valuable part of year round preparation for 100m/200m.
- Some idea of comparative standards is afforded in table 26.

8.70 200m INDOORS

- The banking on indoor tracks is seldom compatible with the speed of 200m athletes. The athlete must practise on banked bends if he wishes to compete indoors seriously. He must learn:—
  - to lean-in without loss of balance.
  - to work more vigorously with the right arm on the bends, and drop the left.
  - to shorten stride on the bend. A fast, light clipped stride is better than a long driving stride.
  - to balance in blocks in the set position on the banking.
  - to work off the first bend and into the back straight before striding.
  - to adjust to *any* lane.
  - to run about 30cm from the inside of the lane.
  - to lift off the last bend and run through the finishing line.
- The coach and athlete should check the track all the way round for consistency of surface, dips etc. On certain tracks there is a dip as a feature of design in lanes 1 and 2 going into and coming out of each bend.
- Indoor/outdoor time difference for 200m is suggested in table 26.

8.80 400m INDOORS

— Broadly speaking, the points for 200m apply in terms of technique.
— The first two bends are in lanes, with athletes breaking for the inside on entry into the home straight for the first time (a line indicates where the break should take place.) (Figure 48)
— The athlete must lift off the second bend to the break point, and work for a fast first home straight into the third bend. He should not look around or be content to follow.

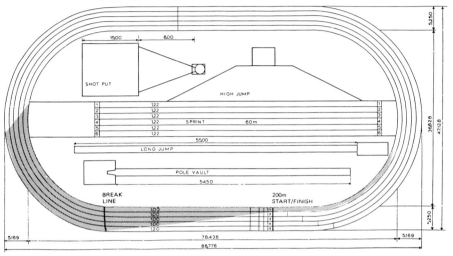

Figure 48

The 400m athlete must apply maximum pressure through the shaded part of the race. -- i.e. into and through the home straight in the first lap. It is *not* the time to wait and see what the opposition is doing!

— On coming off the third and fourth bend, the athlete should let his momentum carry him to the outside of the inside lane.
— The key is a light fast shorter stride on the bends — lifting off the bends, and striding the straights — *but* the second bend and home straight for the first time *must* see the athlete up with the leader or in the lead.
— Indoor/outdoor time difference is suggested in table 26.

8.90 RELAYS — INDOORS

8.91 4 × 200m

— The four legs are as for the individual 200m.
— A standard checkmark should be used of approximately 4.50m for senior men; and 4.00m for senior women. Shorter marks will apply for age groups. The acceleration zone limit line should be used as the checkmark, with the athlete starting 4.50m etc inside the zone.
— The change should be visual. The athlete sprints into the relay box on reacting to the checkmark, then looks round for the baton.

81

— Any of the three types of change may be used, but whatever is agreed *must* be rehearsed as for 4 × 100m.
— The outgoing athlete takes in the left, changes to carry in the right.

8.92 4 × 400m

— The first leg is as for the individual event in terms of lanes. Thereafter the pattern of the run is virtually that of "outdoors leg 3" applied to legs 2 and 3 — and "outdoors leg 4" applied on leg 4.
— The points of technique for the four legs are as for the indoor 400m.
— Particular attention should be drawn to the need for control on accelerations and decelerations in each leg. It is tempting to "kick" on the back straight in the second lap, only to find that the athlete who was passed at that point has far more in his legs in the home straight. The key, as in all 400m, is judicious distribution of effort and pace.

TABLE 26

GUIDE TO INDOOR SPRINT PERFORMANCES

60m

WOMEN	MEN	
7.15 & Under	6.60 & Under	Elite level of World 60m sprinting
7.15-7.20	6.60-6.65	Medal contention in major international championships.
7.15-7.30	6.60-6.70	Top level U.K.
7.30-7.40	6.70-6.75	Finalist contention National Indoors.
7.40-7.50	6.75-6.85	Semi finalist contention National Indoors: Top level U.K. Junior.
7.50-7.90	6.85-6.95	Finalist contention (U/20 men/U/17 Women) National Indoors.
7.50	7.00	Useful "barrier" for sprinters to break.
7.50-7.80	7.00-7.20	Good level U/20 performance
7.60-8.00	7.10-7.40	Good level U/17 performance.
8.00-8.20	7.30-7.60	Good level U/15 performance.

200m
Indoor 200m time is approximately 0.80-1.10 seconds slower than outdoor.

400m
Indoor 400m time is approximately 1.00-2.00 seconds slower than outdoor.

Note: Track design; ambient indoor temperature; track surface, and track sub surface have profound influence on performance times.

9.00 THE SPRINTER'S EQUIPMENT

Competition: *Running Shoes (Spikes)*

— Neat fitting and light.
— Cleaned, dried and aired after competition.
— Laces checked and replaced as necessary after competition.
— Shoes checked for wear after competition.
— The profile of screw-in spikes and elements should be experimented with (e.g. two spikes at front — remainder elements.)
— Spare laces; varying size spikes and elements; and a spike "key" should be carried in kit bag to the competition.
   Thought should also be given to taking a spare pair of spikes in the competition kit bag.
— When a pair of competition spikes are "finished", the athlete should let his physiotherapist see them before throwing them out.

Training Shoes (flats)

— Comfortable and light.
— Cleaned, dried and aired after competition.
— Laces checked and replaced as necessary after competition.
— Shoes checked for wear after competition.
— Spare laces should be carried in kit bag to competition.

Vest and Shorts

— Neat fitting but not restrictive.
— Kept clean and dry for the competition.
— Relevant to competition (e.g. club/team issue)

Socks

— Natural fibres (e.g. cotton)

Underwear

— As comfort and good taste dictate!
— Should be neat, comfortable and "functional".

Extras will include

— Talcum powder
— Towel
— Measuring tape (block spacings)
— Note of block spacings
— Note of relay checkmarks
— 1 dozen safety pins.
— B.A.A.B. Training Diary

Training: *Running Shoes (Spikes)*

— Relevant to the demands of the training unit. (e.g. grass running, bounding, hill running etc.)
— These are *not* simply abandoned competition shoes! The latter may well be useless for training.
  The training spikes must be good enough for the tough task required of them.
— Cleaned, dried and aired after training.
— Laces checked and replaced as necessary after training.
— Shoes checked for wear after training.
— Spare laces; varying size spikes and elements; and a spike "key" should be carried in the kit bag to training.

— When a pair of training spikes are "finished", the athlete should let his physiotherapist see them before throwing them out.

Training Shoes (Flats)

As for competition "flats". However, they should also be relevant to the demands of the training unit if that is an indoor/gym/weights room etc. unit.

Vest and Shorts

These should be clean, dry, comfortable, functional and decent!

Socks

— As for competition equipment.

Underwear

— As for competition equipment

Track Suits and Wet Suits

— Neat, comfortable and "functional".

Athletes should learn early the habit of removing all kit from the kit bag after training; and ensuring that only clean, dry kit in good repair goes back into the bag!

Starting blocks

— Athletes may well invest in a set of personal blocks for training, in the event of there being none at the training venue.

Extras might include

— weights jacket   — elastic rope
— harness   — talcum powder
— measuring tape

| | — B.A.A.B. Training Diary and pencil | — stop watch. |
| | — marking tape | |

Warm-Up: *Running and Training shoes*
— Relevant to competition or training requirements.

Vest and Shorts
— Pre-training — as for the unit of work
— Pre-competition — neat, comfortable and functional. They will become soaked with sweat and the athlete should change into his competition kit prior to reporting at end of warm-up.

Socks
— As for competition and training.

Underwear
— Relevant to competition or training requirements.

Over-wear (e.g. tights, sweat top)
— Preferably made from natural fibres (e.g. cotton, wool)

Track Suit and Wet Suit
— Comfortable and "functional", with a hood.

Extras
relevant to competition or training requirements. Some athletes use leg or ankle warmers throughout warm-up, and occasionally in training, to keep tendons etc., in a warm "envelope".

In addition, the athlete will have, in his kit bag, basic toilet requisites (towel, soap, etc.), and a B.A.A.B. Training Diary.

The Coach's Equipment
Clothing:—
— Adequate to protect against the ambient conditions e.g. *Sunshine:*— shorts, top, training shoes.
Cold :— track suit; wet suit/thermal suit; sweater/sweat top; training shoes/boots; etc.

Supplies:—

— Box of varying length spikes and elements and spike keys.
— Spare laces
— 12 dozen safety pins.
— First aid box
— Marking tape
— 6 relay batons
— Stop watch (preferably with split and memory capability)
— Measuring tape (30m)
— Starting pistol or clapper
— Elastic rope
— Training Diary and pencil

Needs to have access to:—

— Club support

Essential Access:—

— Relevant training venues:— Track
                                          Indoor track/hall
                                          Strength training room
                                          Flat grass/hills etc.
— Physiotherapy and sports medicine advice
— Resource material (e.g. Athletics Coach; Relevant B.A.A.B. Coach Education Programme content and updates; other sprints coaches etc.)

Nice to have access to:—

— Portable video unit
— Home computer
— Sources of supply (e.g. weights jackets
                                        harnesses
                                        speed balls
                                        wrist/ankle weights
                                        wet vest
                                        etc.

10.00 IN CONCLUSION

Although the sprints are the briefest duration events of Athletics' complex of sports, it is most certainly not the case that time and effort in training is less than for other events. A top class sprinter will train almost 4-5 hours per day through the winter, and 2-3 hours per day during his season. The rewards of such labour may only be 1/100's of a second faster or a better placing in a final, but whatever, they are as precious to athlete and coach as any reward in sport. Moreover, to be able to sprint faster holds high premium in many other sports, and the coach who can help his charges to do so is a most valuable and respected resource.

ATHLETICS COACH

The Coaching Journal of the B.A.A.B.

Published:
March, June, September, December

Details from:

B.A.A.B. Coaching Office
Edgbaston House
3 Duchess Place
Hagley Road, Edgbaston
Birmingham B16 8NM

Notes

Notes